How to Restore and Customize
Automotive Interiors

By Dennis W. Parks

motorbooks

D1225770

Dedication

As with my previous upholstery book, I dedicate this book to my wife, Sandy. Hot rod projects and book projects have come and gone over the years, but you have been there all along. It hasn't always been the smoothest ride, but you've stuck with me. Yes, we've learned a lot, including not to attempt to build a hot rod while writing a book about the process. I think I finally understand that.

First published in 2012 by Motorbooks, an imprint of Quarto Publishing Group USA Inc., 400 First Avenue North, Suite 400, Minneapolis, MN 55401 USA

Motorbooks titles are also available at discounts in bulk quantity for industrial or sales-promotional use. For details write to Special Sales Manager at Quarto Publishing Group USA Inc., 400 First Avenue North, Suite 400, Minneapolis, MN 55401 USA.

To find out more about our books, visit us online at www.motorbooks.com.

Cover: The restorers at Griffin Interiors have transformed the interior upholstery of this old classic.
Photo courtesy of Team Killeen

ISBN-13: 978-0-7603-4247-3

Library of Congress Cataloging-in-Publication Data

Parks, Dennis, 1959-
 How to restore and customize automotive interiors / Dennis W. Parks.
      pages cm -- (Motorbooks workshop)
 Summary: """This guide helps automotive hobbyists and automotive shop employees better understand how to customize the interior of a vehicle. The book features over a dozen projects with hundreds of photos and step-by-step instructions"--Provided by publisher"-- Provided by publisher.
 ISBN 978-0-7603-4247-3 (pbk.)
 1. Automobiles--Interiors--Maintenance and repair--Handbooks, manuals, etc. 2. Automobiles--Customizing--Handbooks, manuals, etc. I. Title.
 TL275.P27 2012
 629.2'6--dc23
                                        2012010905

President/CEO: Ken Fund
Group Publisher: Bryan Trandem
Publisher: Zack Miller
Editor: Jordan Wiklund
Design Manager: Brad Springer
Designer: Trevor Burks

Printed in USA

Foreword

When I first started reading this book, I did not have a good knowledge of how to work with upholstery. In the past I have worked on every other skill required to repair, rebuild or build an automobile but not upholstery. Now, after reading this book, I am ready to try my luck at learning a new skill.

When I attend car shows and cruise nights, it seems that the topic always comes up: where do I take a car to get it upholstered? You hear many stories about inferior work, and high prices, and it scares the potential customer. Suppose you have your car upholstered, and it does not turn out the way you wanted, or not the quality that you expected, and the shop charged more than you planned–now you have spent your money and you do not have the finished product you wanted.

This book has taught me about what to look for in a high quality job. I often ask the owner of a car that I am looking at, "where did you get your car upholstered?" His answer, and my summation of the work on his interior, helps me evaluate the shop that did the work.

In my area there is a very limited number of quality upholstery shops. The good shops are expensive, and they have a backlog of business. I have also heard the term, "Upholstery Shop Purgatory." This is the case when your car enters the shop and just sits there forever with little or no work being done. All of this makes want to try to learn

this new skill and upholster the car I am currently building for my wife.

I have made a quick calculation of what would be required for me to give upholstery a try. By sheer luck I have a chance to acquire a quality sewing machine and I have most everything else I need except for a few specialty tools. I know I will make mistakes but it appears to me that any mistake you make could be redone. It would take additional materials and time, but it would be possible to simply go back to the beginning and start over. I am thinking that the cost of the materials and tools, and the wasted time in redoing mistakes, would still enable me to save money over paying a shop to do my car. This type of work is labor-intensive and that is where much of the cost adds up.

I plan to carefully evaluate all of this information and make a decision. I really like the idea of doing a job like this myself. I like the feeling you get when you finish all the work on a custom project. Reading this book has given me the knowledge and the encouragement to give upholstery a try. I hope it does the same for you.

—John Kimbrough
Lifelong hot rodder &
Bonneville Land Speed Record Crew Chief

Acknowledgments

About the same time this book, my eleventh for MBI, was submitted, my tenth book, *Automotive Wiring*, became available. Although I was always interested in writing when I was growing up, I never dreamed of becoming an author. As this book is published, I hope my readers and MBI allow me to write even more. Thank-you to everyone at MBI, past and present, for making this partnership a success. I hope we can work together to publish many more books.

Something that will make this book even better than my previous upholstery book are the photos showcasing various sequences from start to finish. Obtaining those photos required contacting trimmers who knew what they were doing, allowed me to photograph them and their shops while they were working, and answered all my silly questions. I say thank-you very much to Jerry Klitch and Brian Flynn at Sew Fine Interiors. Jerry and Brian are consummate professionals in their approach to upholstery and made me feel welcome the entire time I was in their shop. They continued with their work as if I were invisible and completed several how-to sequences in relatively few days.

Other trimmers I have worked with over the years contributed to this book in one way or another. In no particular order, I thank Chris Smith at CarSkinz Custom Auto Interiors, Joan and Ed Thornton, Don Albers, Jack Waller, Shawn Appleman at Appleman Interiors, and Sam Wright at Sam Wright Hot Rod Interiors.

Most importantly, thank-you to everyone who reads my books and especially those who shell out hard-earned money to buy them. I sincerely hope you have enjoyed and learned from them, as I know I have. Wishing you the best success in your upholstery endeavors.

—Dennis W. Parks

Introduction

Many people are interested in working in the automotive aftermarket but do not desire to work as a mechanic or in a body shop. Engines and mechanical systems are constantly changing, so in addition to remembering how to diagnose, service, and maintain older vehicles, mechanics must regularly attend classes to hone and upgrade their knowledge base for newer vehicles. In addition, the multitude of makes, models, and manufacturers requires a hefty toolbox—a handful of wrenches just won't cut it anymore. Skillful bodywork is no longer as necessary as it used to be because most damaged body panels are now simply replaced and refinished rather than repaired. The volume of cars is increasing while the volume of skilled mechanics and body workers is decreasing.

Nonetheless, many people desire to work with automobiles, either as a full-time job or just as a hobby. Automotive upholstery is a rewarding automotive field, one that can be mastered on the job, doesn't require extensive training beyond the basics, and doesn't require a semi trailer full of tools. As with any profession, it is good to work at an established shop for a while, so a mentor can assist in your training. An existing business also gives you the opportunity to work on a wide variety of upholstery styles in an equally wide variety of automobiles.

By the time you finish reading this book, you'll have a good grasp of the basics of restoring automotive upholstery. A logical next step might be to purchase a seat of relatively simple design from a salvage yard and to reupholster it. If that salvaged seat doesn't turn out well, you can always redo it. If it does work out, you may be tempted to try your hand at a real-world application: your own car. Not only will the work be more rewarding, it will stand as a working example of your new skills and will give you the confidence to set up shop in your own garage. It may even be enough to help you land a job at an established body shop.

No matter which course you choose, this book is the place to start. In Chapter 1, we'll discuss tools and materials—basic, but you need to know it. Chapter 2 discusses sound-dampening and thermal insulation materials. If someone is going to the trouble and expense to reupholster a vehicle, it makes great sense to minimize unwanted noise and to get the most from the HVAC and stereo systems. We'll get our hands dirty in Chapter 3, as we learn how to remove seats from a vehicle, repair them, recover them, and reinstall them. Chapter 4 teaches you more than you thought you would ever need to know about interior door panels, while Chapter 5 shows you how to cover the floor beneath them. In Chapter 6, we'll introduce you to both traditional and sculptured headliners and teach you how to design and upholster both types. Chapter 7 discusses treatments for secondary interior spaces of the automobile. Finally, an appendix explains how to care for your "new" vehicle interior.

If you feel automotive upholstery is for you after reading this book, take a class at a tech school or a community college to learn how to sew. With that skill and the information here, all you need is a little experience to become a competent trimmer. You'll never look at a vehicle the same way again.

Customizing an automotive interior is one of the most rewarding projects for car lovers.

Chapter 1
Tools and Materials

In any profession, craft, or hobby, there are certain tools to become familiar with; automotive upholstery work is no different. The tools you need, and the amount you need to spend, depend on how involved you want to get. But if you are going to do the job right, having the right tools is crucial, and being able to provide a superior product will no doubt make your efforts more rewarding, both emotionally and financially.

You will also need to learn about the various materials associated with automotive upholstery. Some upholstery materials have been around for a long time, while others are being developed and improved every year. It is necessary to know which materials are used for which tasks and which materials can or cannot be substituted if you run short of something in the middle of a job. Some materials are expensive and therefore raise the overall price of a job without increasing your amount of work. Leather and high-quality vinyl look and feel much the same, but leather is much more expensive than its composite cousin. Which should you choose?

This first chapter will answer this question, as well as many more. In the chapters that follow, you'll learn about several distinct portions of the automotive upholstery process. In the beginning, it is best to work on small projects that can be completed in a short time, so you do not get overwhelmed. Each project offers a variety of challenges, and each will give you more experience. Some projects provide an opportunity to try a different approach to the same task, so you can determine which method works best for you. After all, it's all about customization.

TOOLS

The two most expensive items generally needed for upholstery work are an industrial sewing machine and an air compressor.

A sewing machine, a pair of shears, a tape measure, and a pair of hog ring pliers are the most commonly used tools. Most upholstery work involves merely cutting material into smaller pieces and then sewing it back together to make a bigger piece.

They are readily available and can be one-time purchases if you shop around, find what you need, and pay for what you need the first time. That doesn't mean you must buy the most expensive sewing machine and air compressor available, but if you spend the money now, you'll avoid spending more later. You might be able to get by with something less than ideal for a while, but it is better to spend the extra money up front. A new air compressor typically costs between $400 and $800, while a new industrial-quality sewing machines typically costs between $700 and $1,000. Both of these pieces of equipment will last for a very long time if properly maintained.

Most of the other required tools can be found at a local hardware store or through a wholesale supplier of upholstery materials. Among these are tools for layout, cutting, and fastening. There are multiple methods for doing the same task, depending on which tools you have access to. It is possible to start with a pair of scissors, a tape measure, and a pair of hog ring pliers to install a simple seat cover, but you'll need more tools as you complete more jobs and gain experience.

Among the most basic and frequently used tools are the ones for measuring and layout. Because humans do not have calibrated eyeballs, you'll need something to measure with, something to draw straight lines with, and something to make sure that lines and edges are square with each other. These tools are available at your local hardware store or home improvement center. You'll also need chalk and china markers to indicate cut marks, pleat lines, and other information on the material you are working with. These items are available at any art supply store.

Measuring Tools

An 8- or 12-foot tape measure should be suitable for most upholstery jobs, although more advanced projects might require a 16- or 25-foot measure, or longer. In some instances, a carpenter's steel tape or a dressmaker's cloth tape work better. You can find a cloth tape wherever you purchase fabric.

An important note about tape measures: whenever you are laying out pleats or anything that should be parallel, use the same measuring device on both ends. Tape measures are rarely wrong, but over some undetermined distance, a steel tape, a cloth tape, and wooden ruler might have some slight variance among them. You don't want to sew a bunch of pleats into a piece of material only to realize that they are 1/16 inch narrower on one end than the other. You might not notice this difference on a couple of pleats, but you sure will all the way across a bench seat. It's more important to use tools with consistency than with the truest measure.

Layout Tools

To lay out straight lines, such as pleats or edges for door panels, you will need a straightedge. It can be made of wood or metal (aluminum is common). An advantage of a metal straightedge is that you can cut against it with a razor knife.

If you use wood, over time a razor knife will cut into it, and eventually the straightedge won't be quite straight. Although it might be too cumbersome for some tasks, an aluminum T square, such as that used with gypsum drywall, is beneficial if you require multiple lines that are square with one another.

Marking Tools

For marking pleats, reference lines, or simply an outline for where to cut material, chalk or a china marker is commonly used. A china marker works best on vinyl or leather and can

A 25-foot tape measure will be more than adequate for most auto upholstery jobs.

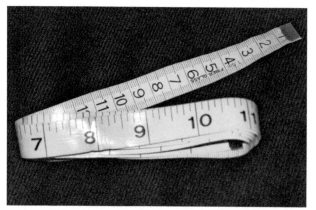

Some trimmers prefer a cloth dressmaker's tape measure to a steel tape, simply because the former does not retract if not locked into position. Either style of tape measure will work, so the decision is simply a matter of personal preference.

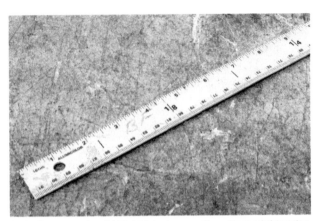

An aluminum measuring stick/straightedge is commonly used in an upholstery shop. As a measuring tool, it works well to lay out pleats or to repeat measurements. As a straightedge, it can be used to draw lines on foam or fabric. It can be used with a razor blade or utility knife when cutting thin material. This particular straightedge is marked in yard sections, as fabric is commonly sold by the yard.

The square shown is a smaller version of a typical carpenter's layout square, but it serves the same purpose. It is useful for verifying whether pleats are perpendicular to a seat base or for any other instance where something needs to be square to an adjacent edge.

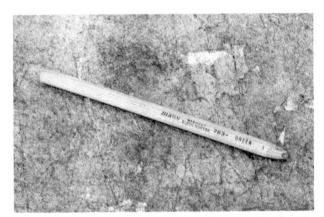

A china marker is useful for marking pleats, reference lines, or any other information on vinyl, leather, or another fabric with a slick finish. The markers are available in multiple colors; your toolbox should have at least one dark color and one light color. The marks typically remain on the surface indefinitely but are easily removed with 3M's General Purpose Adhesive Cleaner.

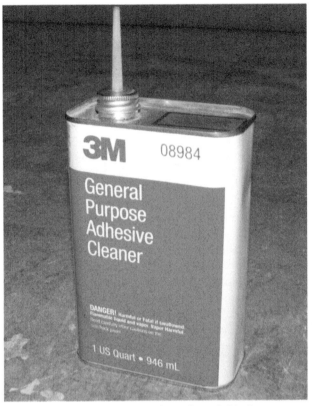

Designed for removing adhesive overspray from various materials, all-purpose cleaning products work well to remove china marker or almost any other substance that may end up on your upholstery material. Simply pour a little bit on a paper towel or cloth and wipe the material gently to remove the mark.

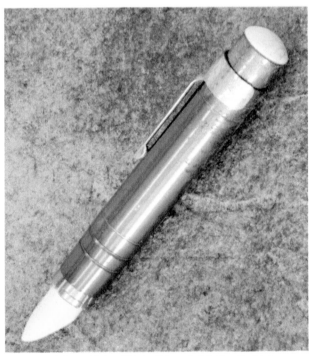

You can use chalk on cloth-based fabrics. Using a chalk holder will minimize breakage and also keep chalk dust off your fingers.

be cleaned off with 3M's General Purpose Adhesive Cleaner applied to a paper towel or soft cloth. Chalk works best on tweed or cloth materials; avoid using chalk on vinyl or leather, as the grit in the chalk can cut the material slightly.

Cutting Tools

Upholstery work requires you to cut a collection of small pieces of fabric from a larger piece and then to sew or glue them together. Most fabrics are sewn together, although backing material is commonly glued on. Regardless of how components are attached to each other, they are first cut to size, making cutting tools a necessity.

Depending on the thickness and density, foam material can be cut with scissors, a razor knife, or a band saw. A foam knife may be necessary to cut foam thicker than approximately 1/2 inch. A less expensive option is to use an electric carving knife from the kitchen. It will eventually fatigue under this kind of abuse, but it can be replaced several times for the difference in cost.

ABS door panels can usually be scored on the back with a razor knife and then snapped along the scored line. Wood-based door panels may require a woodcutting saw equipped with the appropriate amount of teeth for the material. More teeth give a finer cut, but cutting takes longer. As long as you exercise patience and don't rush the process, most wood-based or ABS door panels can be cut using a power jigsaw or scroll saw. Relatively thin (1/8 inch or less) lauan wood paneling can be cut with a razor knife. If you are cutting pieces that need to have exact straight edges, it might be easier and less time-consuming to use a razor knife along a metal straightedge than to draw a line to follow with a saw, which then has to be followed with a file to achieve the required precision edge.

Shears: Some trimmers call them shears; others call them scissors. Regardless, they are the common tool for cutting most upholstery fabrics. You should avoid cutting staples or wire, as doing so may knick the blades, leaving a knick in each piece of material cut thereafter. With upholstery shears, you really get what you pay for; more expensive shears usually feel more comfortable in your hand and feature cushioned grips. You will be using shears often and sometimes for long periods, so comfort should be a prime concern when purchasing a pair. Shears work best when sharp, so high-quality shears that maintain their edges are essential. A good rule of thumb is to keep at least two decent pairs of shears, so that a freshly sharpened pair is always available.

Knives: Knives and razor blades are typically used for cutting relatively thin materials. Sometimes they are used to cut freeform shapes. Other times they are used against a metal straightedge to cut (you guessed it) a straight edge in the material. They are also used to cut apart seams when removing old seat covers for repair or replacement.

Saws: Saws are commonly used for materials that are too thick to be cut with shears or a knife or for rigid materials such as panel board or medium-density fiberboard (MDF). Saws in an upholstery shop usually include some sort of saw for cutting foam and a jigsaw or scroll saw for cutting irregular shapes. An advanced upholstery shop will have woodworking equipment to construct center consoles, stereo enclosures, door panels, and seat bases. In this kind of custom work, a table saw, a circular saw, a scroll saw or jigsaw, a belt sander, and a router or edger will be put to good use. Safety glasses and ear protection are always required when working with power saws.

Trimmers use shears on a daily basis, so spend money wisely. Shears have a blade of 6 inches or more, while scissors' blades are less than 6 inches long. Whichever you choose, purchase two pairs that are well balanced and fit comfortably in your hand.

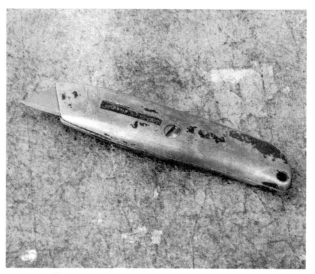

A common utility or razor knife is indispensable for cutting panel board, carpet, and various other materials around the upholstery shop.

Industrial Sewing Machine: A heavy-duty, industrial-quality sewing machine is necessary for sewing automotive-grade upholstery material. This kind of machine can be found at an upholstery supply store. Do not expect to use a typical household sewing machine to sew upholstery-grade material.

Most trimmers use a single-needle, dual-foot machine with both forward and reverse sewing capabilities. Although a reverse feature is not an absolute necessity, it makes locking the beginning and ending of seams easier. This type of machine uses a full spool for the top thread and a smaller bobbin for the bottom thread. Two presser feet help keep the material properly aligned while you sew. One is located beside the needle and is referred to as the sewing foot. A second foot, located behind the needle, is referred to as the dual feed foot. A serrated bar called a feed dog is located under the needle. In synchronization with the needle, it moves up under the fabric and pulls the fabric forward one stitch. Some machines use a walking needle (or walking foot), which moves forward one stitch as it passes through the fabric and, in combination with the feed dog, pulls the fabric forward.

Air-Powered Tools

Air compressors can be used in a wide variety of applications, but for upholstery projects they work in conjunction with spray guns, drills, and pneumatic staplers. Other pneumatic tools, such as sanders and grinders, are used for the woodworking aspects of upholstery work. Rather than a heavy-duty air hose designed to be driven over and able to withstand other extreme shop conditions, a lighter-weight, self-coiling air hose works fine for upholstery, if you work in an area not subject to vehicular traffic. If complete vehicles will be driving into your workspace, a heavy-duty air hose is required.

Razor blades are commonly used for cutting apart seams, trimming excess material, scraping glue off glass, and cutting almost anything else that requires a sharp edge. Be sure to use single-edged blades in the garage; keep the double-edged blades safe in the bathroom.

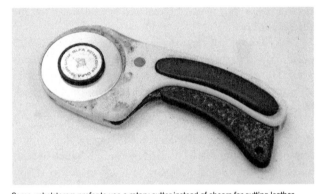

Some upholsterers prefer to use a rotary cutter instead of shears for cutting leather and some vinyl materials. This tool can cut more accurately around patterns, which minimizes waste material. You squeeze the handle as you move the tool along. Working much like a pizza cutter, the round blade moves downward and cuts the material.

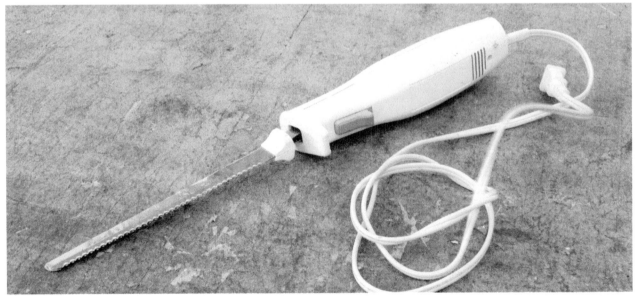

Commercial foam cutters are expensive. A more affordable alternative is an electric carving knife designed to cut ham and other meats in the kitchen. The blade will need to be sprayed with silicone lubricant on a regular basis. Just don't use the one from your wife's kitchen unless you buy her a new one.

A large worktable and a gooseneck light are important accessories for a sewing machine. Leading brands of industrial-quality sewing machines are Consew, Brother, and Singer.

Air Compressor: A 60-gallon tank and 3- or 4-horsepower air compressor is the minimum you should consider. This size is ample for a one- or two-person workshop. Commercial shops have larger and more powerful air compressors, but you won't need anything industrial strength.

If you are going to use a stationary air compressor, consider installation of a piping system with a water trap or air dryer at the end. Though not as critical in upholstery work as in painting, dry air is beneficial to the life of your pneumatic accessories. For home use, a small air supply system with 3/4- to 1-inch pipe is advantageous. A copper or galvanized pipe running downhill, away from the compressor, allows moisture accumulations in heated air to flow from the compressor to a trap or dryer. Since the hot air has time to cool inside the pipe, moisture suspended in the air condenses into droplets, which are captured and retained in the trap.

Spray Gun: An expensive spray gun is not recommended; save that for repainting the house. You are going to be using a spray gun mainly for applying glue, so don't spend extra money for a top-of-the-line model. The gun will need to be cleaned on a routine basis with the appropriate cleaner, and eventually it will need to be replaced. If you need a spray gun for applying paint (to seat frames or door panels, for instance) or other refinish materials, purchase a different spray gun. Don't use the one you have for spraying glue.

Pneumatic Stapler: Since you already have an air compressor, you might as well benefit from a pneumatic stapler instead of a more labor-intensive manual stapler. From fabricating custom bucket seats to replace factory ones to making sculptured door panels and elaborate center and overhead consoles, a pneumatic stapler is a handy tool because much of this work requires covering.

A pneumatic reciprocating saw, commonly known as an air saw or a Sawzall, is indispensable for any fabrication work, such as making consoles or stereo boxes. This type of saw allows you to cut freeform shapes.

Staples are available in a variety of lengths. You need a staple of adequate length to firmly attach the fabric to the panel, but not one so long that it completely penetrates the panel and punctures the fabric on the other side. During the course of any complete vehicle upholstery job, you'll need staples of several different lengths, so stock up on all sizes.

Fastening Tools

After you have cut, sewn, glued, and accomplished any other tasks for your custom seat cover or door panel, you will need to secure the material to the seat frame or door. Most but not all seat covers are secured in place with hog rings. Hog rings are similar to extremely heavy-duty staples in that they puncture material to hold it in place. The difference is that rather than flattening out against itself, as a staple does, a hog ring closes around a wire or rod in the seat frame.

In the early 1900s, many vehicles had wooden substructures. Wood was an easy and logical attachment point for upholstery panels, which were secured in place with small nails or tacks. Magnetic tack hammers with relatively small heads (compared to framing hammers) were used to secure the tacks to wooden tack strips or wooden substructures. Tacks are mostly no longer used, but you may encounter some that need to be removed when reupholstering a vehicle built in the early 1900s. Magnetic hammers are very useful, as most of the tacks are quite small. You can simply attach a tack to the hammer and drive it in place, rather than attempt to hold the tack with your finger and thumb, as with larger nails.

To remove and reinstall seats, you'll need a variety of combination wrenches or ratchet and socket wrenches. You'll need a variety of screwdrivers to remove and replace all the screws you may encounter, including Phillips, slotted, Torx, and others. Each vehicle inevitably requires the purchase of at least one more tool for your collection.

An air nozzle that can be connected to your air hose is great for erasing chalk marks from fabric. It also comes in handy for removing other dust and debris from a project upon completion.

Two kinds of spray guns are common: one utilizes an integral material cup, and the other utilizes a remote material cup. The latter is referred to as a pressure pot, as adhesive or another material is transferred from the pressurized pot through a hose to the nozzle and then blown out the nozzle by the air supply.

Use a pneumatic stapler for securing fabric (vinyl or cloth) to the back of panel board or MDF. Be sure to use staples of appropriate length so they do not pierce the material on the front face.

WORKING SPACE

A large, flat table or workbench at a comfortable height is ideal for upholstery work. Whether you will be sitting or standing is for you to decide, but the worktable should be at a comfortable height for both. Quite often, an upholsterer's table is positioned at a comfortable height for standing, with a stool rather than a chair used for sitting. You might sit some of the time, but you will be standing a lot at first. Investing in a workstation floor mat to reduce fatigue is not a bad idea.

The table should be at least big enough to roll out the largest piece of material you'll be working with. In most cases this will be a headliner, which might be 6 feet wide, or for some vehicles close to 10 feet long. Lots of table space won't always be necessary, but when it is, you'll be glad to have it. The worktable should be covered with thin cardboard or Masonite to provide a smooth surface. The covering should be inexpensive, so you don't have to spend a fortune to replace it when excessive wear and tear begin to show.

Many newer hog ring pliers are spring-loaded, which means the hog ring can be placed in the jaws and it will remain there until it is squeezed in place. With this feature, you can set the loaded pliers down to pull material into place without the hog ring falling out of the pliers.

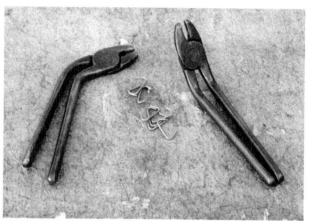

Back in the day, hog ring pliers were used in most upholstery jobs to secure seat covers to seat frames. Some had straight handles. Many of today's models have bent handles to better reach into difficult locations.

A tack hammer has two small faces, one of them magnetized. Old-time trimmers placed tacks in their mouth, picked one up with the magnetic end of the hammer, and tapped it into place. After the tack was started, the trimmer spun the hammer around and finished driving the tack with the nonmagnetized face.

Many snap buttons, such as those found on convertible tops and tonneau covers, are installed with rivets. To use a manual rivet gun, spread the handles and load the rivet shaft into the opening of the gun. Position the rivet where you want it. Then squeeze the handles together to drive the rivet into place.

Since a big table will leave a substantial footprint in your shop, use the area below the work surface as storage. Rolls of material can be stored under the table at one end, with accessories such as nuts, bolts, and seat hardware in storage bins at the other end. How much storage space you require depends partially on how you run your shop. If you complete one job before starting another, you won't require room to store additional seats and their related hardware. If you take on multiple projects at once, you'll need a larger workspace.

Your workspace will require at least one large table for laying out fabric prior to cutting it. The layout table should be at a comfortable working height, so you don't have to bend over and strain your lower back. If room is available, a second table for disassembly/assembly of seats and other components is a valuable asset.

This well-equipped woodworking area includes several worktables around the periphery and a dust collection system. A table saw for cutting foam and panel board and an edger for rounding the edges on panels can be seen. Also shown are a collection of commercially available templates for door panels, seat cushions, stereo speaker enclosures, and a multitude of other shapes.

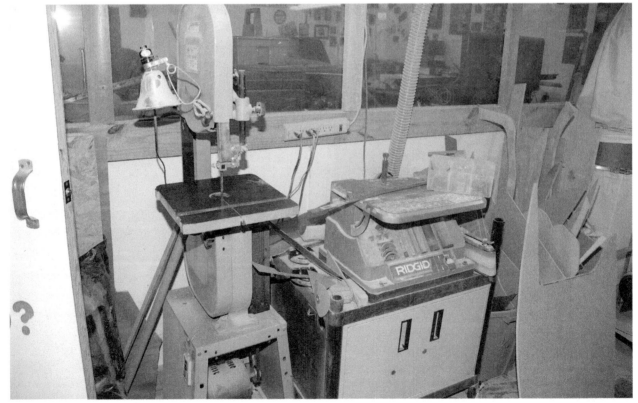

If you build center consoles or sculptured door panels, or use woodworking power tools for any other reason, limit this work to a specified area. This will keep dust and debris from getting in the rest of your shop and onto upholstery materials.

OTHER TOOLS

Pliers, wire cutters, ice picks, and small weights are also necessary for upholstery work. Pliers and wire cutters are used to remove old wires, hog rings, and nails that secure old upholstery to seat frames. Ice picks, awls, and similar devices are used to align multilayer door panels during construction.

Tack pullers are used for removing tacks, staples, and other fasteners. When removing original upholstery, keep the original fabric intact, so it can be used as a pattern. The comb-type puller show here is versatile, as it can be used with staples of varying width.

An ice pick or awl is also useful for poking small holes in carpeting when searching for seat- or seatbelt-mounting holes in the floor. Small weights, such as chunks of lead or beanbags, are sometimes needed to hold material to a panel while contact adhesive is drying. Whatever you use for weight, make sure it is reasonably soft and has no sharp edges that could damage material.

Other tools that may be required as your trimming experience grows include heat guns, specialized clip removal tools, and paint equipment. Heat guns are used to soften material, smooth out wrinkles, and remove glued-on emblems from door panels and other interior panels. When using a heat gun, be sure not to concentrate too much heat in one place, as you might do more harm than good. Several different types of retaining clips are used throughout the automotive industry, and they are almost impossible to remove unless you have the tool designed to remove them. Different manufacturers use different tools. Figure out what you'll need ahead of time, and spend the few bucks necessary, to save yourself headaches (and possibly larger expenditures) later in the process. Anytime you start an upholstery project, be sure to check whether you'll need any special tools. Factor the price of the tools in with expenses for the job.

If you are going to be painting interior pieces that require something other than what is available in a simple spray can, you will need a paint spray gun. You won't need a high-quality gun like that used for automobile painting, but a good spray gun with air and fluid adjustments will come in handy.

Diagonal side cutters can be used like tack pullers, as well as for cutting wires and staples. You'll quickly become accustomed to the most common tools in your arsenal. Over time, you might acquire several specialty tools, depending on the type of work you are doing.

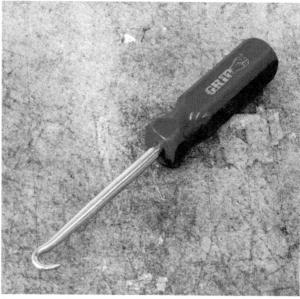

Occasionally it may be necessary to remove cotter pins or to pull springs onto or off a bracket. A hooked tool such as this one makes doing so possible (and usually easier).

Shown are two commercial tucking tools (top and bottom) and one improvised tucking/sculpting tool (middle). These are most often used for installing headliners. The improvised tool is merely a piece of wooden dowel with a slightly rounded end and an eyebolt threaded into the opposite end. These different radii are used to push fabric into recesses in sculpted panels.

A laminated section of foam makes a good storage location for fitting pins, tufting needles, and curved needles. Fitting pins are typically 2 to 3 inches long with a loop at the end. They are used to align multiple panels to ensure that the pattern lines up properly. Tufting needles are used to hand sew buttons in a seat cushion or seat back. Curved needles are primarily used for blind stitches or to repair ripped seams.

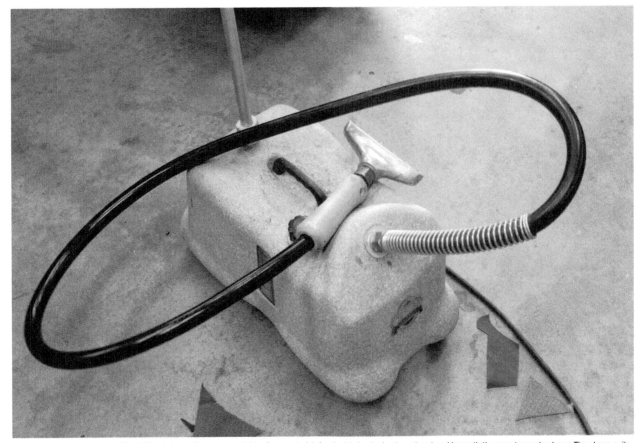

A steamer is a trimmer's best friend. Steam is used to remove wrinkles from material. An electric heater heats water stored beneath the case to create steam. The steam exits through the nozzle at the end of the hose.

MATERIALS

As with tools, materials will vary, depending on what you are covering and how you are doing it. Depending on the surface and the desired result, you may or may not use padding. You will then cover the surface with the desired material.

Padding Material

Padding material (foam) is typically available in three distinct types: open cell, closed cell, and molded. Each type has its own uses and characteristics.

Open-cell foam is probably the most common type of foam associated with automotive upholstery. It is fairly soft. While small quantities can be purchased in precut sheets, open-cell foam is usually sold in rolls and is available in several different thicknesses, commonly ranging from 1/4 inch to 4 inches. Thicker material is also available, but it is not commonly used in automotive applications. If you need thicker foam, you can simply glue together multiple layers of thinner foam to create the desired padding. Thin open-cell foam can be cut with a sharp razor knife, but thicker foam usually requires a foam knife or band saw. Open-cell foam is used for seat cushions and seat backs. Bolsters are made by gluing additional foam around the front and sides of a seat

Rollers of various sizes and contours are used for pushing sound-dampening and insulation material into the contours of sheet metal floor pans. They are also used to push material into recesses of sculpted panels.

Commercial trimmers typically purchase foam and fabric adhesive in bulk, but it is also available in spray cans. You should apply the adhesive to both surfaces and allow it to become tacky before pressing the materials together. If you don't allow the adhesive to become tacky, the material won't stick, resulting in bubbles.

Silicone spray is used to lubricate the blades of shears or foam knives, and also on the inside of seat covers to make them slide more easily over seat cushions.

cushion and around the top and sides of a seat back. The foam must be cut to the shape of the seat before it is covered.

Closed-cell foam is similar to open-cell foam in that it is available in different thicknesses, can be glued together to form layers, and is usually sold in rolls. The two types of foam differ most greatly in their compressibility. While open-cell foam is easily compressed, closed-cell foam is more difficult to compress because of its density. Closed-cell foam is commonly used to pad headliners and door panels, or in situations where sculptured patterns are being used. When sculpting foam panels to be covered with fabric, avoid tiny, intricate shapes in the foam; they are difficult to adhere to the fabric. Instead, use larger, more sweeping shapes, so that the upholstery material is more easily worked into the crevices of the pattern.

Closed-cell foam also has a relatively slick surface, due mainly to its manufacturing process. To ensure that upholstery material adheres to it properly, scuff the surface slightly with 80-grit sandpaper to allow the adhesive to properly soak in.

When using open-cell or closed-cell foam, fabric is glued or sewn to the foam. If you are sewing directly onto the foam, it must have a backing to prevent the thread from simply pulling through. Use scrim-back foam or use glue on a layer of muslin as a backing.

Open-cell foam is most commonly used for automotive upholstery. It is much more compressible than closed-cell foam and is dense enough that it can be shaped with a knife to create seat bolsters and cushions of various shapes and sizes. It can also be glued into layers to create shapes and thicknesses not commonly available.

On the left is 1/4-inch-thick open-cell foam. On the right is 1/2-inch-thick open-cell foam. Either of these could have material sewn or glued to them. For repairing or modifying a seat cover, new material is sewn to 1/2-inch-thick foam and then sewn to the rest of the seat cover. Material is glued to the foam to give a bit of padding to a console, dash, armrest, or door panel.

The third type of foam is molded foam, which is very similar to closed-cell foam. Molded foam is injected into a mold of the desired shape. When the molding process is completed, the foam is the correct shape and size of the seat. It is usually then attached to a framework and upholstered with the desired material. Molded foam is quite dense and provides firm support while maintaining its shape. Seats for most late-model vehicles are made with molded foam. Additionally, a growing automotive aftermarket offers reproduction seat cushions for some popular older vehicles. If you are restoring a vehicle that has replacement cushions available, this will be the quickest method of restoring the seats to their original condition, whether you use OEM-style fabric to cover them or not.

SEAT AND DOOR COVERINGS

Seats and door panels can be covered in just about any type of material. Vinyl, tweed, leather, and even blue denim have been used by auto manufacturers. Some materials look much better than others; it simply depends on personal style and the demands of the car.

On a period-perfect hot rod roadster or pickup truck, an Indian or Mexican blanket hog-ringed to the seat frame, with the excess folded nicely, looks just as appropriate as the finest leather on a fully restored Rolls-Royce. Simply throwing that blanket over the seat, however, without neatly folding the corners or securing it to the frame with hog ring pliers, will look like an unmade bed. If you are going to succeed as a professional trimmer, your work must be neat, regardless of the material used. The quality of your work is up to you and will reflect your attention to detail.

Closed-cell foam is typically used on door panels, quarter panels, and headliners to provide a slight amount of padding, or in any situation where sculpturing is going to be done. Closed-cell foam is far denser than open-cell foam and is not as compressible. A thicker piece will condense more than a thinner piece but still not as much as open-cell foam.

Although material used for upholstery should be on par with the materials and workmanship on the rest of the vehicle, there is a wide price range with seat upholstery materials. The following prices are current as of the writing of this book and are all from the same source. Unless noted otherwise, all materials are 54 inches wide. Standard vinyl upholstery material—a high-quality alternative to leather, with excellent durability and available in a variety of colors—wholesales between $20 and $30 per square yard. Tweed upholstery material that is similar to wool also runs between $20 and $30 per yard, depending on color. Tweed probably has the widest selection of colors from which to choose. A little higher up on the price list is contract cloth material, which wholesales between $25 and $30 per square yard. Next, soft-touch vinyl material wholesales between $25 and $40 per square yard. This material is manmade and resembles various exotic leathers at a fraction of the cost. Ultraleather HP, a manmade leatherlike material, wholesales between $60 and $100 per square yard. It is virtually as durable as leather, somewhat softer, and slightly less expensive. Ultrasuede HP runs between $80 and $125 per square yard. For real leather, expect to pay between $6 and $10 per square foot.

Yes, leather is priced per square foot instead of per square yard. A square yard is the same as nine square feet. Thus, a square yard of standard vinyl costs about $20, while the same amount of leather costs between $81 and $135. Always take into account the cost of different materials for your upholstery projects.

In addition to cost, leather has another drawback. Manmade material comes in exact widths by whatever length is needed. Real leather comes in the shape of the animal, be it a cow, ostrich, or snake. Unless you take shape into consideration and carefully plan the patterns of your interiors, using animal skins can result in lots of waste (and therefore lots of expense).

Regardless of the material, the methods and the labor will be the same. The quality of the material and its price are what make the big difference on the cost of a trim job. A high-quality vinyl or cloth is significantly less expensive than the same work completed in leather.

Leather

If you are trimming a one-off custom vehicle where money is no object, leather or leather alternative shows that extra bit of style, comfort, and elegance. Real leather feels good on your skin and carries a pleasant aroma, making it ideal for covering the interior of a high-quality automobile.

Some vehicles are upholstered with nothing but leather, but they are the exception rather than the rule. With the high quality of certain imitation leathers, such as Ultraleather HP, you can achieve the look and feel of leather without spending quite as much money. But if you must have some real hides in your vehicle, you can cover the bulk of the interior in vinyl and incorporate smaller accent panels of cow, reptile, ostrich, or other exotic skins.

Unknown to the majority of the car-buying public, a common practice among original equipment manufacturers (OEMs) is the leather-vinyl match. The top of the seat cushions and the front of the seat back are upholstered in leather, but the rest of the seat is covered in a matching vinyl. This is a much more affordable option if a complete leather overhaul isn't necessary.

Vinyl

Vinyl has received a bad rap as an upholstery material because of low-cost vinyl seat covers sold through mail-order or other discount retailers. Vinyl is not an inferior product, but many "one size fits all" universal seat covers simply do not fit properly. The material used in these seat covers is not necessarily the best, but it is the poor fit that causes the problems. If the installer does not purchase the best-fitting seat covers and secure them properly in place, they will move around during normal use, causing them to look bad and wear out prematurely, leaving everyone involved unhappy.

High-quality vinyl upholstery material is available. When not abused, today's vinyl materials provide years of good service and sometimes even pass for leather. Vinyl is available in almost any color and in various weights and thicknesses. Marine-grade waterproof vinyl is designed for use aboard watercraft but is not a suitable choice for an automotive interior.

Cloth

Cloth is frequently the standard upholstery material in OEM vehicles. Available in a wide range of colors, patterns, and textures, cloth is quite versatile. However, its application is more common for restoration or repair of OEM seating and interiors than for custom upholstery projects. That is not to say that cloth cannot be used for a custom project.

HEADLINER MATERIAL

Material used for headliners is very similar to material used to cover seats. The big difference, if any, is that the headliner material is lighter in weight. Since the headliner material is hanging, gravity affects it, making lighter material a better choice. Heat is also a factor, so some headliner material is perforated to allow it to breathe more easily.

Binding and Edging Material

Edging material includes cording used to make piping to trim the seams of upholstery work. Binding material is used to cover the piping. Cording is always covered, so it is typically some neutral color. Binding material is available in a wide variety of colors to match the same variety of upholstery colors, however, using a variety of colors calls for a different roll of binding material for each color of seat cover material. A more contemporary approach is to simply purchase enough extra of whatever material you are using so that the piping is an exact match to the rest of the upholstery.

A sample ring of leather in a wide variety of colors. Leather is extremely soft when properly treated. It can become hard and stiff if not properly cared for.

Vinyl fabric is available in a wide variety of qualities and colors. Each type of vinyl has different characteristics, making it suitable for some uses and not others. Determine which type of material is most suitable for your project.

Velour, cloth, and similar materials are usually used in restoration projects to match the original upholstery. When reupholstering a vehicle to improve it, vinyl or leather is more common.

Single-fold binding material is used to cover seams where different pieces of material are joined. The binding material is wrapped around a piece of cord and sewn to hold the cord in place. The flaps are sewn to the two pieces of material that are being sewn together.

Cording is available in different sizes, but 1/8 inch in diameter is commonly used for automotive upholstery, with slightly larger sizes used in household furniture.

Interior Design Gallery

Walking around a car show can provide many ideas for automotive interior designs. Whether you are an amateur or a professional trimmer, you will want to make each interior at least slightly different from others done in the past. Many professional shops alter their custom designs, even if a customer asks for the same treatment as his friend. Checking out new vehicles will give you new ideas.

In this competition-oriented coupe, racing seats are fully upholstered with pleated vinyl. Thicker foam provides more definition of the pleats, while thinner foam provides less definition.

This vintage pickup features a heavily modified dash as well as a center console. Bucket seats, door panels, and the console are all covered in similar material. Custom inserts match the paint on the dash.

This pickup truck includes a mostly stock dash and high-back bucket seats from a donor vehicle. The pleated pattern is not difficult and makes for a good first-time project.

The pleated vinyl seat in this '67 Chevrolet pickup is similar to the stock seat cover. The difference is merely the higher-quality material used in the restoration and the addition of the Chevy logo in the middle of the seat back.

This Model-A Tudor includes aftermarket seats, easily installed by a trimmer. Making this interior unique is the zebra print fabric used to cover the door panels and the floor.

Light tan vinyl or leather complements the orange paint on this roadster nicely. The darker brown covering over the floor console provides a fine contrast to the light-colored interior. Notice the humorous inserts in the seat backs.

The body of this roadster has been modified to closely surround the backs of the bucket seats. Door panels are three dimensional and provide depth to the interior.

In the same vehicle as above, we see a mysterious control panel built into the seat cushion. This is a roadster. It does not have power windows and most likely does not have power door locks. Based on the perforations within the chrome or stainless trim strip, the five toggle switches might be controls for a hidden stereo.

In this custom interior, a chrome or stainless-steel trim strip extends from the front near the floor, across the door panels, across the back of the seat, and to the opposite side. The ignition switch is nestled under the dash at the top of the center console.

I'm sure this convertible had a bench back seat when it rolled out of the factory, but custom buckets serve just as well. Let's face it, back seats in automobiles are not expected to be as roomy as they once were. The inserts of exotic leather skins add character to the otherwise nice but somewhat plain interior.

Many hours went into this vehicle's upholstery. The front seats have been restitched. They might have come from another vehicle or might be completely custom. I suspect that the back seats are custom-made to match the fronts. The center console is a one-off creation, and the pattern of the door panels extends to the back seat area. Oh, and it is a convertible too!

Chapter 2
Sound Dampening and Thermal Insulation

Whether you are simply re-covering the interior of a factory-built vehicle or upholstering a frame from a restoration or rebuilt vehicle, installing sound-dampening material and thermal insulation is a good idea. And now, while the seats are out of the vehicle, is the time to do it. Even if the vehicle has OEM insulation, higher-quality material is available and should be used. Some OEM insulation is glued in place; some is held in place by the mounting of the seats. If after removing the seats, you cannot easily lift the insulation out of the vehicle, use an old putty knife to scrape it up.

Insulation material will not help if the structure of the vehicle has significant air leaks. You must eliminate excessive holes in the body. Repair them by welding in patch panels or even by replacing body panels if the holes are significant. Other than rust holes, holes are most commonly found in the firewall where electrical wires or heater hoses enter the passenger cabin from the engine compartment. Previous owners may have added additional holes, some of which may no longer be needed. For holes that are needed but have

excessive clearance around them, use foam to seal the gaps. Incomplete welds and missing seam sealer allow air leaks. In these cases, apply seam sealer (automotive caulking available from automotive paint and supply stores).

Carpeting and insulation might hide some rust-through in floor pans (including trunk floors and wheel houses). If you find rust-through or other damage to the vehicle's substructure, you'll need to address it before doing any upholstery work. The last thing you should do is simply install insulation and carpet over floor pans that are in need of repair.

If the floor pans suffer from only surface rust, you can remove it with a Scotch-Brite pad and repaint the surface with rust inhibitor. Be sure to follow the directions, use the correct primer, and allow for proper drying time before installing any insulation or carpeting. If the floor pans are in good shape, use a mild solvent or liquid dishwashing soap and water, along with a scrub brush, to clean them. Once a solid floor pan is clean, you can begin installing sound-dampening and insulation material.

Fiberglass bodies are not as susceptible as steel bodies to noise caused by vibration, but sound dampening is a good idea, even in an open vehicle. This Dynamat sound barrier is a heavy rubber-coated material, easily cut to shape with scissors. Once the backing is peeled off, the sound barrier is pressed into place.

SOUND DAMPENING

Regardless of quality or cost, all automobiles generate noise. As a vehicle's engine runs, energy is transferred throughout the vehicle, causing vibration. This vibration is turned into noise throughout various sheet metal components, such as a car's doors, floor, and roof. Even if these components are made of fiberglass or other composites, they still act as sounding boards for vibration. (Note that throughout the book, I will use the term *sheet metal* to refer to such body components, regardless of their materials or construction.)

Though vehicle noise cannot be totally eliminated, it can be managed considerably. OEM automotive designers use acoustic materials in the engine compartment to minimize drivetrain noise, in the passenger cabin to minimize wind and road noise, in the trunk compartment to minimize road and exhaust noise, and elsewhere.

Unwanted noise can be minimized by dampening and absorbing. Dampening involves lining body panels, door panels, floor pans, and roofs with material that is acoustically "dead." To work efficiently, this material should cover at least a third to a half of the interior sheet metal. Some builders cover the entire interior with this material. Common sound-deadening material comes in the form of a self-adhesive, dense, rubberized asphalt mat, weighing a pound or two per square foot. For more on installing sound-deadening material, refer to the "Installing Sound Dampening" project on page 34.

Minimizing noise by absorbing involves soaking up sound waves and preventing them from reflecting back into the vehicle. Absorbing is accomplished by installing dense fibrous material with open pores, such as open-cell foam or fiberglass. Thicker materials typically absorb a wider range of noise frequencies; thinner materials typically absorb only medium and high frequencies.

THERMAL INSULATION

In addition to noise, all engines create heat. Since most engines are in front of the passenger compartment, with the exhaust system beneath the passenger compartment, a fair amount of heat builds ups beneath the vehicle. Heat rises, so there needs to be some insulation between passenger and engine.

A foil-faced heat barrier is one type of thermal insulation. It can easily be cut to shape and glued in place.

The climate of this '68 Chevy pickup is greatly enhanced by the addition of a Dynamat foil-faced heat barrier. Not only does the heat barrier help keep out ambient heat or cold, it makes it easier for your heater or air conditioner to keep the car's interior at the desired temperature.

After cutting the heat barrier to the correct size and shape, glue it in place. Apply spray adhesive to the floor (or the vibration dampener, if used) and to the back of the heat barrier. Allow the adhesive to become tacky on both surfaces and then press the heat barrier in place.

A relatively thick, fibrous material or open-cell foam should be applied on the floor and the firewall to minimize heat transferring to the inside of the passenger compartment. This same material helps keep ambient heat from entering the car on a hot day and heated air from exiting on a cold winter day. Thermal insulation can be applied to other surfaces, but at the very minimum it should be applied to the floor and firewall.

MATERIAL OVERVIEW

Dynamat and HushMat are two leading brands of sound dampening and thermal insulation (see "Resources" at the end of this book for contact information). Both brands offer similar products; sample both brands to determine which products work best for you.

Dynamat Xtreme and HushMat Ultra are both sound-deadening and vibration-dampening products. They are available in sheets of various sizes, are self-adhesive, and are very flexible, allowing them to be easily shaped to the contours of the inner sheet metal of a vehicle. Both products are used primarily where heat is a factor, such as on the floor or firewall, but they can be used on doors, side panels, and trunk floors as well.

HushMat Silencer Megabond is an absorber product applied atop HushMat Ultra. It is commonly used on the floor to absorb exhaust, road, and wind noise in the 600- to

Dynamat Xtreme can be used to reduce noise caused by vibration and as a heat barrier. This product is available in different size sheets and can be cut to fit with a utility knife. It is also self-adhesive.

4,000-Hz noise frequency. Dynamat Dynaliner is a single-layer, foam-type, heat-blocking insulator available in 1/8-, 1/4-, and 1/2-inch thicknesses. Applying either Hushmat Silencer Megabond or Dynamat Dynaliner to the inside of doors provides a noticeable (3- to 6-decibel) reduction in road noise. Covering the trunk and roof further reduces the amount of road noise inside a vehicle. If a specific panel is causing vibration-induced noise, apply a vibration-dampening product to that panel or to an entire surface area to minimize the resonance.

Dynamat DynaDeck is a floor liner. It can even replace carpeting in a roadster or other open car susceptible to moisture from weather or washing. It is composed of a 3/8-inch-thick waterproof liner over a 1/4-inch-thick layer of high-efficiency, thermo-acoustic foam. DynaDeck features an embossed vinyl top.

HushMat Quiet Tape is a soft, pliable foam tape that can be used to secure wiring harnesses and cables to floors, side walls, and trim panels. Unlike duct tape, which will eventually dry out and fall off, Quiet Tape will last indefinitely.

Dynamat DynaSpray is designed to protect hard-to-reach areas. It is a sprayable, water-based ceramic coating applied to inner and outer door panels and inner and outer fenders. It can also be used as undercoating. It comes in a flat black color but can be painted to match or contrast with your color scheme. Applied with a brush, roller, or product-specific spray gun, DynaSpray requires 48 hours to fully cure.

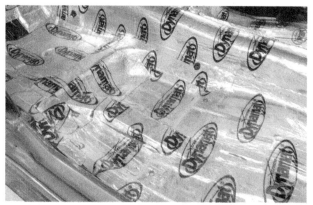

For best results, self-adhesive sound-dampening and heat barrier materials should be fully pressed into the contours of the surface to which they are applied, including recesses in floor sheet metal.

To spray this material inside of doors, make sure the windows are fully shut and remove the interior door panels. Door- and window-mechanism access holes vary in size from one vehicle to another, but you should be able to spray most of the inside of the exterior door skin by directing the spray through these access holes. Spray a layer of undercoating approximately 1/8-inch thick. Thicker coatings may leave residue on door glass as it moves up and down.

Avoid getting any spray undercoating on the interior of the door or on the window riser mechanism. On metal parts,

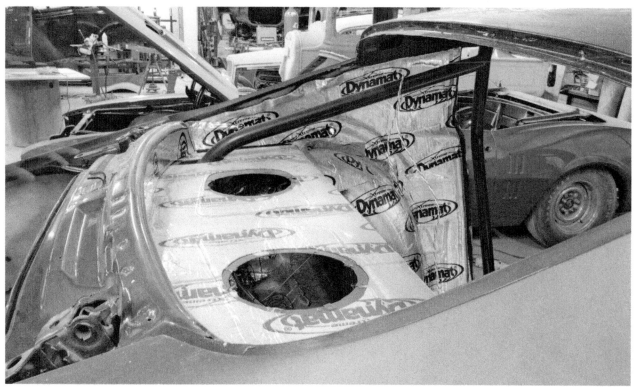

Sound-dampening material should be cut around speakers to obtain the truest and best sound from your stereo system.

the undercoating can be removed with a bit of kerosene on a cloth.

Spray-on undercoating can also be applied to the inside of fenders. To spray the inside of rear fenders, remove the lining of the trunk if your vehicle is so equipped. This is very easy to do with most vehicles; the trunk lining simply sits at one end and is held in place with plastic bolt-like fasteners at the other end. Most fasteners are removed by turning them counterclockwise. Remove the fasteners and pull the trunk lining out of the way. Like the bare door panels, the fenders have access holes. Apply the undercoating in layers up to about 1/8-inch thick. It isn't necessary to let the undercoating dry like paint material, but may want to leave the trunk lining off until you are finished undercoating the entire vehicle. This allows you to see if you missed any spots. When you are finished, reinstall the trunk lining.

Front fenders usually don't have any sort of lining, but there may be other obstacles to contend with, such as a battery, windshield washer reservoir, or other engine-related items. Each vehicle is different. Which obstacles can be easily removed and which ones cannot varies greatly. The decision should be left to the trimmer or person applying the undercoating. Some undercoating products have a flexible hose attached to the nozzle, which makes application into difficult-to-reach areas somewhat easier.

HushMat Ultra H2O Paste is a water-based, air-drying body seam sealer applied with a caulking gun. After it dries, it can be sanded and painted, but that is not required.

Almost any surface you have access to is a good candidate for Dynamat or HushMat, but for best results, the material should be applied to the insides of doors, the trunk, and floor areas first. If you choose to install more, apply it to the interior panels of the rear deck, roof, hood, and fenders.

You can also buy insulation material cut specifically for a certain vehicle. This is undoubtedly the easiest material to install, as it is already the correct size or at least close. Sometimes it only needs to be trimmed to allow for specific options, such as a floor console or shifter.

When installing any insulation material in a vertical panel—such as the inside of a door or quarter panel—do not let the material extend all the way to the lowest point of the cavity. Any moisture that enters this area (such as rainwater or spilled liquid) could be soaked up by the insulation material and become a source for rust.

This vehicle uses relatively cheap foil-faced bubble wrap as a heat barrier. Better results are obtained with HushMat or Dynamat. Since bubble wrap loses its efficacy if the bubbles collapse, limit its use to areas that will not be subject to foot pressure.

INSULATION INSTALLATION

Sound-deadening insulation is available in relatively small sheets that easily conform to the irregular contours of a car's floor. A sample installation of this type is shown on page 34. Many absorbing types of insulation are thicker and come in larger sheets. These are a little more trouble to handle due to their size.

Begin by measuring the overall length of the interior compartment of your vehicle, including the firewall and the panel that separates the passenger compartment from the trunk area. Cut a piece of insulation material slightly longer than that measurement. For reference, use a piece of chalk or other marker to indicate an approximate centerline of the insulation front to back, so that the insulation fully covers from side to side. You may need to fold the insulation to get it into the vehicle. With help from someone on the opposite side (if available), push or pull the insulation as needed, so that it is centered front to back and side to side.

Secure the insulation with adhesive, such as 3M's Top and Trim Adhesive. This is a contact cement, so it must be applied to both surfaces and allowed to become tacky. Then push the material into place. It is probably easier to begin in the rear portion of the vehicle due to the lack of a transmission hump. Fold the back half of the insulation onto the front half and spray adhesive onto the floor or the sound-deadening insulation (if already installed). Also spray adhesive onto the bottom side of the back half of the insulation. Unfold the insulation and begin pressing it into place along the front-to-rear centerline of the vehicle, working your way outward. Once you are satisfied that the insulation is located properly, trim the insulation material away from seat mounting tracks or seat belt mounting holes with a sharp utility knife. Take your time and smooth out any bubbles or wrinkles. If they are not removed at this point, they will show up later when carpeting is installed. You can trim the edges now or wait until all the insulation is glued down.

With the back half of the insulation installed, fold the front half of the insulation back. Spray adhesive onto the front half of the floor and the bottom of the insulation. Press the insulation into place, again working your way forward and from the middle. Depending on the size and shape of the transmission hump in the front of the passenger compartment, you might want to cover this sometimes difficult area last and with separate, smaller pieces of insulation. It is common on vehicles with large transmission humps to use three pieces (one over the hump itself and one on each side). After the majority of the insulation is glued, trim the edges as necessary, apply more adhesive to both the floor and the insulation, and press the insulation into place.

On vertical surfaces and on the inside of roofs, a heavier application of spray adhesive is necessary to hold the insulation material in place. The adhesive still must be allowed to become tacky before the insulation is pressed into place. Car tops get very hot in the summer sun, so adhesive used to apply insulation material to the inside of a car roof should be labeled "high temperature," with a rating of at least 160 degrees Fahrenheit.

CERAMIC INSULATION

Another popular insulation is LizardSkin ceramic insulation. This insulation is perhaps most suitable for specially constructed vehicles (as they are being built) or complete rebuilds that have been gutted on the interior. This liquid coating can be applied to a vehicle that is already finished, but the extensive disassembly and masking required may prove to be impractical for some applications.

LizardSkin ceramic insulation is a water-based composition of air-filled ceramic and silica particles. The particles combine with acrylic binders, similar to paint products in consistency. LizardSkin ceramic insulation claims to reduce engine and solar heat transfer by 25 to 30 degrees or more. It also serves to reduce noise by as much as 10 to 12 decibels.

Since LizardSkin ceramic insulation is a liquid, it can be applied to any clean and dry-primed or painted rust-free surface. For best results, LizardSkin should be sprayed on. Prior to application, uncoated areas must be masked off with masking paper or masking film (available at automotive paint and body supply stores). Ambient temperatures must be 70 degrees Fahrenheit or above. Apply LizardSkin ceramic insulation in thin coats; it takes three or four coats to achieve the desired thickness of 0.040 to 0.060 inch (about the thickness of a credit card). LizardSkin ceramic insulation must fully dry between coats (the dry finish will be flat and dull). Curing time before sanding or additional finishing is 24 hours at 70 degrees or warmer.

WEATHER STRIPPING

It may be necessary to replace weather stripping around doors and windows. Replacement weather stripping can be purchased in kits for some vehicles and in bulk for most vehicles. If the weather stripping around the doors needs to be replaced, run a piece of tape or draw a line around the old weather stripping, to indicate where it fits properly, prior to removing it. Pull the old weather stripping off, using a putty knife if necessary to loosen hard-to-remove areas. Fit the new weather stripping around the door to check for length and to verify that the placement between the door and the body is correct. Apply a bead of weather strip adhesive to the backside of the weather stripping per the manufacturer's instructions. Some brands need to become tacky; others don't. Place the weather stripping into position and allow it to dry before operating the vehicle. Many installers use strips of masking tape to hold the weather strip in place while it is setting up. Wipe away any excess adhesive.

PROJECT 1
Installing Sound Dampening

  Time: 1–2 hours

 Skill Level: Easy

 Cost: Low

Tools & Materials: Insulation material, heat gun (optional), roller, generic household cleaner

If you are redoing an interior, this is the perfect time to add sound dampening and thermal insulation. The basic steps are only slightly more involved than those required to reupholster seats. First, remove the seats and any floor mats, carpeting, insulation, or padding. Vacuum or sweep out any foreign objects that have found their way to the floor pan. If any parts of the floor pan are rusted through, the holes need to be repaired. After cleaning the floor pan, the sound-dampening material can be installed. To gain insight into this process, follow along as Brian Flynn of Sew Fine Interiors finishes the job on a mid-1960s Plymouth Fury.

Brian was almost finished installing HushMat in this vehicle, but I caught him in time to see how it is done. Notice how the insulation material tightly conforms to the shape of the floor's sheet metal, including the indents in the panels.

The insulation material is self-adhesive, but the surface must be clean and free of grease. Use a spray-on household cleaner to clean the surface. Wipe off any residue.

Relatively small precut sheets are easier to work with than one large sheet that would need to be trimmed to fit. Peel off the protective backing.

Use a heat gun to make the material a little more pliable. If you do not have access to a heat gun, lay the insulation material in direct sunshine for a while before using it.

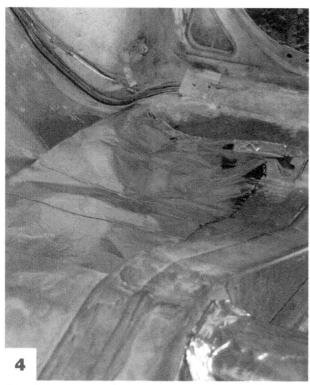

4

Pick up the insulation material and set it in place with the foil side up. Smooth out the obvious wrinkles with your hands, picking the material up slightly and repositioning it if necessary.

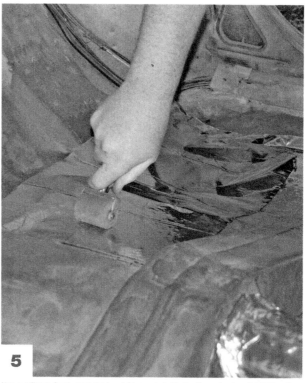

5

Use a roller to firmly seat the insulation material to the floor sheet metal. Follow the shape of the sheet metal as closely as possible, including any reinforcing ribs. Make sure you have rolled the entire surface of the insulation material before moving to the next piece.

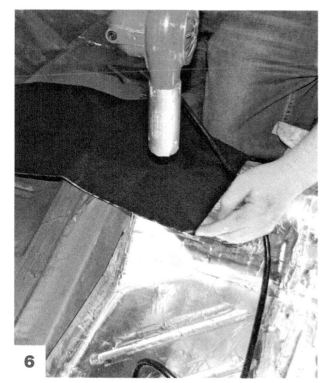

6

Cut the next piece to the correct size and shape, peel off the protective backing, and heat it slightly to make it more pliable.

7

Press the insulation material into place and roll out any wrinkles. Continue until the job is done.

Chapter 3
Seating

When you are finished with the upholstery work on a vehicle, it should all look nice, but the seats should also be comfortable. If the seating is not comfortable, the upholstery work no longer matters. No matter how straight your stitches or how even your pleats, the job is a failure. If people cannot sit comfortably in the seats for up to two hours, you should reconsider the choice of seats. Understanding the importance of comfort as well as craftsmanship puts you ahead of the game.

SEATING OVERVIEW
While it's not necessary to be an ergonomic engineer to upholster seats, it helps to have a little knowledge of the human body and its muscular system. In all likelihood, any seat that originally came from a mass-produced automobile or is designed to fit into a mass-produced vehicle can be made to work for your project. You might have to lower the seat to provide a bit more headroom or raise the seat to increase visibility. The seat might need to be moved forward or backward slightly beyond its adjustable range so that a petite driver can better reach the pedals or a pro basketball player does not have the steering column in his chest. Adding a bolster to the sides or front of a seat, or even just additional padding, might make driving or riding much more comfortable for someone who has had hip or knee surgery. On the other hand, the bolsters of that sports car might need to be removed so that the older—but wiser—driver can more easily get out of the seat.

A new covering is not going to make a seat any more comfortable, so now is your opportunity to fix that. Foam cushions are relatively inexpensive, so even a basic seat recovery job can be accomplished on a tight budget. Now is the time to verify exactly what it is you're looking for and how much it will cost.

Old seats aren't completely useless. You can use the old covers as patterns for cutting new material. If all you're doing is replacing the covers, simply sew the new material together, slip it over the seats, and secure it in place. It's usually not that easy, though. Most likely, a spring will need repair, foam will need replacing, or at least one portion of a seat cover will be torn too badly to use as a pattern.

The steps required to reupholster a seat are broken down in greater detail in the following pages, but the general procedure is as follows: remove the seats from the vehicle; remove the existing covers; assess the condition of the seat frame, springs, and cushions; make repairs as necessary; cut out and sew new covers; install and secure the covers; reinstall the seats in the vehicle.

REMOVING SEATS FROM THE VEHICLE
Seats (or their adjustment sliders) are typically held in place with four bolts. The bolts pass through the floorboard into threaded inserts or nuts welded to the underside of the floor pan. Sometimes four studs are welded to the floor, and the seat or adjustment sliders fit over the studs. The seat is secured by threading a nut onto each stud. The nuts, inserts, or studs are welded to the floor pan, you can remove (or reinstall) seats without having a second person crawl beneath the vehicle to hold a wrench. If a nut or stud turns while you are trying to loosen the seat mounting bolts, it must be re-welded to the floor pan.

When removing seats from a vehicle, make notes about how they are secured. The safest place to keep the seat mounting bolts while the seats are out of the vehicle is in the threaded inserts or on the threaded studs that they came from.

The underside of this bucket seat shows the mounting brackets and sliding adjustment. Note that the rear mounts are taller than the front mounts. This difference will not present a problem if the seat is reinstalled in the same vehicle it was taken out of, or in a similar one, but if the seat were swapped into a vehicle with a flat floor pan, it would lean forward.

Before you simply unbolt and yank seats out of a vehicle, check to see if any electrical connections for power or seat heating must be disconnected. From the factory, these connections are typically plugs that can be easily disconnected and reconnected. However, if anyone has done repair work to the vehicle involving the seats, he might have connected the wires individually. In this case, make notes about the connection before you disconnect any wires, so that you can reconnect them properly when you are finished with your work.

REPAIRING OEM SEAT FRAMES AND SPRINGS

Whether you have taken the covering off an old seat or are working with a new aftermarket seat frame, make sure it is clean and in good condition. An aftermarket seat frame will probably just need to be wiped off. An older seat frame might need substantial work before it is ready to be upholstered. You will need to remove any bird's nests, rat's nests, animal droppings, and animal remains, especially if the vehicle is a barn find. This advice may seem silly, but most any automotive upholsterer can give a detailed account of one of these situations or worse.

Remove any unnecessary hog rings, staples, or other wires that may puncture upholstery material. Check to see if any springs are loose. If so, they should be resecured to the framework. Verify that the sliding mechanism works smoothly. Damaged or bent tracks will need to be straightened or repaired. Verify that the seat back folds smoothly if it is supposed to fold. Take a few moments to remove dust and dirt. Apply a bit of lubrication (silicone or another substance that will not stain or otherwise damage new upholstery) to get the seat frame working properly. If the seat frame or springs have surface rust, remove it by lightly sanding the metal. Heavy rust may require media blasting or a coating of naval jelly or other rust dissolver. To keep rust from reoccurring, spray a coat or two of primer with a rust inhibitor. Follow that with a couple coats of gloss black paint. This will have the seat frame looking like new.

Adding and Replacing Padding

OEM replacement seat foam is available for some vehicles and will make short work of replacing existing foam. However, replacement foam is not available for all vehicles. The cost of a new replacement may overshadow the minor amount of foam that needs to be replaced. If you are replacing only small sections of foam, foam of similar density to the old foam can be glued in place with contact cement and then shaped to the desired contour. If you choose to be creative, you can add multiple layers of open-cell foam to shape the seat cushions and seat backs to your specific design. Each layer of foam can be glued to the previous layer with contact cement. Remember that contact cement or spray adhesive must be applied to both surfaces and allowed to become tacky before the two pieces are pressed together. Not applying adhesive to both surfaces

Analyze the seats to determine how many separate pieces of material you'll need for a seat cushion or seat back cover. This seat back has two pieces for bolsters, along with three separate pieces for the center, and this is just the front side of one seat. From this photo, we cannot tell about the back, but I suspect that the sides and back are all one piece. The seat cushions have four separate pieces, plus one to three pieces covering the front and sides.

In addition to several separate pieces of material, this interior utilizes a variety of stitches and materials. The double row of stitching along the vertical bolster is a French seam. Most everything else appears to be sewn with a topstitch. In addition to the brown vinyl or leather, exotic leather inserts are prevalent. The same material used for the floor covering is used as an insert in the door panel.

and not allowing adhesive to become tacky are the two most common mistakes made by new trimmers.

Additional foam is typically placed into the lumbar region in the seat back. It may also be desirable to add a bolster around the edges of the seat cushion and seat back. The foam is glued together to the desired thickness and then cut to the desired shape with a razor knife. For more on adding foam, refer to the "Building Bucket Seats" project on page 45.

Making Patterns

If the existing covering of the seat you are re-covering is in fairly decent shape, you already have a pattern for the new seat cover. With a razor blade, carefully rip the seams out of the existing cover until you have a collection of individual pieces. While "ripping the seams" may be the correct terminology, you are not actually ripping anything. The goal is to cut each stitch that holds the various pieces of material together. In a sense, you are unsewing the seat cover. Now that the pieces of seat cover are two dimensional rather than three dimensional, they can be used for patterns.

If the existing seat cover is stretched excessively or is too damaged to use as a pattern, you will need to make a new pattern. You can use Kraft paper, poster board, or even scrap upholstery material to make new patterns.

Prior to making the pattern, determine how to actually cover the seat, how many pieces you need, and how they will be sewn together. Being able to visualize the finished product makes crafting the pattern much easier. Consider whether the entire seat cover will be made of the same material or if you will use a complementary or contrasting color or a different type of material. Using more than one color or type of material makes designing the pattern a bit more complicated, but it is also more rewarding.

Some basic seat cushions, whether bench or bucket, have one piece of material that covers the actual sitting area and a second panel that runs forward from the middle of the rear, runs forward on one side, wraps around the front, and runs to the middle rear on the other side. This design requires a seam at the top edge of the seat on three sides. The seat back for this type of cover has one piece of material on the front, another on the back, and a third running from the bottom on one side, upward and over the top, and then down the other side. Additionally, a seam secures the front panel to the piece that makes up the sides and top; another seam secures the back panel to the piece that makes up the sides and top. Each seam usually has matching or contrasting piping or a French seam.

Another style of seat may have the front panel continue down to cover the front of the seat. This design requires separate side panels be stitched to the top and front. Likewise, the seat back needs a center panel that extends from the base of the seat back up and over the top, then down the front to the base. Two separate side panels are attached at the back, top, and front edges.

Since reupholstering a seat requires several pieces of material to be sewn together and the material often changes direction while sewing it, it is critical to make several reference marks while crafting the patterns. Some trimmers cut small notches in the material. Others use chalk marks (often accompanied by numbers). Do whatever works, but make sure you have some way to verify that everything lines up correctly. When sewing, most trimmers line up the centerlines of the material and sew toward one end. Then they return to the centerlines and sew in the opposite direction to the other end. If you simply start sewing at one end, alignment will most likely be less than desirable.

Before you make a one-time-use pattern out of flimsy material, think ahead. If you expect to do a similar vehicle with similar seats or door panels in the future, use a more durable material for the pattern. For example, let's say you upholster many '69 Camaros or '32 Fords. While the seats vary slightly from one vehicle to another, they are all similar, so having durable patterns made of poster board or another sturdy material will save you time (and headaches) in the long run. The costs of higher-quality material will be offset by the time, money, and energy it would take to make the same pattern over again out of cheap material.

To use the same pattern on each of a pair of bucket seats (or to simply make the pattern symmetrical), establish a vertical centerline (left to right) on the seat cushion and the seat back. Measure the seat cushion and the seat back to verify that the centerline is in fact in the center, then mark it with chalk, china marker, or another marking device. It is always a good idea to establish the centerline before the seat cushion and seat back are disassembled from one another, to ensure that pleats or other designs in the upholstery align from one to the other. Whether the seat being recovered is a bucket seat or a bench seat, disassemble the seat assembly so that the seat cushion and seat back are two separate items (unless you're working with a one-piece seat—mostly used in competition-inspired vehicles). Mark a corresponding vertical centerline on whatever you are using as pattern material.

Seat Cushions

Measure across the back of the seat cushion. On the pattern, mark a line perpendicular to the vertical centerline and transfer the dimension—draw a line of the same length and angle--of the back of the seat--onto this line, keeping half of the length on each side of the centerline. Now measure the front-to-back length and angle on the seat and transfer it to the centerline.

The seat cushion cover on these bucket seats wraps down to cover the front of the seat cushion as well, with each side covered by a separate piece of material. By my count, the seat cushion is covered by no fewer than seven separate pieces of material. The seat back has at least six pieces of fabric.

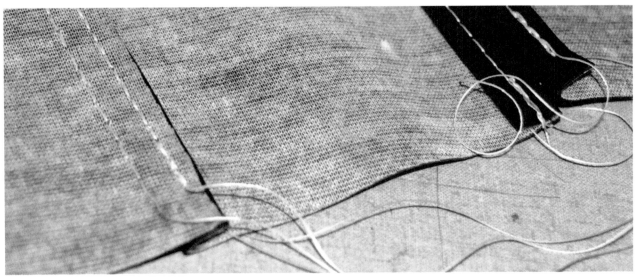

Looking at the back of the fabric, a typical topstitch is shown at the left, with a French seam shown at the right.

From the vertical centerline on the seat cushion, measure to the front corner of the seat. Transfer this measurement to each side of the centerline from the front center of the pattern. Measure from the back corner of the seat cushion to the front corner and transfer this measurement to the pattern on each side. Now connect the dots with a pencil or marker. If you have followed the procedure correctly, the pattern will be the same size and shape as the top of the seat cushion. Before cutting, add approximately 1 inch of material outside of the cushion area around the entire pattern. This extra gives you the necessary material for stitching. If the sides and front of the seat are going to be the same height, measure the overall length and make a rectangular pattern of the same length and cut. Be sure to add 1 inch on all sides before cutting.

SEAT BACKS

Make a pattern for the seat back using the same basic procedure. The big difference between the pattern for the seat back and the seat cushion is that the seat back needs a front and back in most cases. The seat cushion needs a top but does not require a bottom.

To better envision the final look of the pattern described above, imagine placing one flat-bottomed paper grocery bag over the seat back and another over the seat cushion. Each crease in the bag is a seam, unless you choose to make the sides and top of the seat back or the sides and front of the seat cushion from one single piece each.

There are several different types of seats and several ways to upholster each of them, so describing how to make a pattern for all of them is impossible. Just remember to disassemble the seat cushion and seat back if they are indeed two separate pieces (some bucket seats are just one piece). If a bench seat has split backs, the pattern for each back needs to be made, whether they are removed from the seat or not.

Remember to measure twice and cut once, as some bench seats are split 60/40 rather than 50/50. Make patterns for folding armrests and headrests in a similar fashion.

With all your patterns made and cut to the correct size (with approximately 1 inch extra on all sides), place them on your material. They should not overlap but should be placed close to one another so as not to waste much material. Trace around each pattern piece with chalk or china marker. Pieces that are identical can be cut using the same pattern. Just be sure you cut out enough pieces and that they are properly

In this particular seam, the stitching is not visible from the outside, so more stitches (approximately eight per inch) are used to provide a stronger seam. Red thread on red leather makes the stitches difficult to see but has nothing to do with whether the stitches are visible in the finished piece.

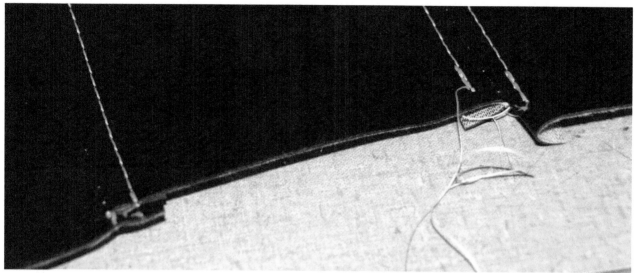

Looking at the front of the same piece of material, the topstitch is again shown at the left and the French seam at the right. A topstitch provides a bit of visual overlap, with one stitch being visible. A French seam will appear as though two pieces are butted together, with two stitches being visible.

oriented. For instance, you might have to flip a pattern to create a piece for opposite sides of a seat.

Cutting Material

After tracing all your patterns, use a sharp pair of shears to cut out each piece of material. When cutting leather, some trimmers use rotary cutters, which are more accurate than shears. With the additional cost of leather, minimizing scrap is no doubt a good thing.

When used on a seat cover, most upholstery material requires foam backing. This gives the seat cover more thickness, making it more durable. It also gives more definition to the pleats or other patterns on the seat cover.

Unroll foam material of the appropriate thickness onto your worktable. Place each piece of material onto the foam, leaving some space between each piece. Cut the foam so that it is slightly oversize when compared to the upholstery material.

Fold each piece of material approximately in half. Then spray the foam with adhesive. After the adhesive becomes tacky, press the material firmly into place and work out any wrinkles with your hands. Repeat the process with the other half of the material. When each piece of material has been glued to a piece of foam, sew around the perimeter of each piece of material. Use a pair of shears and cut off the excess foam. You are now ready to start sewing the pieces together to form your seat cover.

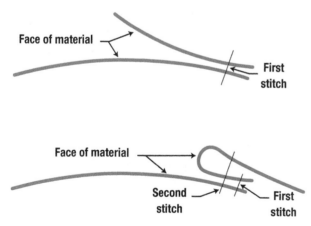

To sew a topstitch, place two pieces of material face to face with the common edge of both pieces aligned. Sew them together, with the sewing machine's presser foot running along their common edge. Then fold one piece of material over so that both faces of material are right side up. Sew through all three layers with a second stitch. (Note that illustrations are not to scale and are shown in exploded fashion for clarity.)

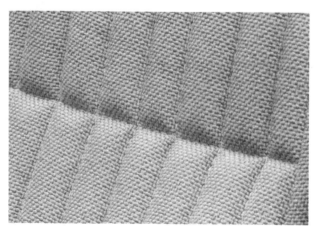

A topstitch can be used to simulate pleats or to create a pattern in an otherwise plain panel. Without stitches to create definition, the seat back would have no real shape or design.

MAKING THE SEAT COVER

If the seat cover (cushion or back) has any sort of pattern (vertical or horizontal pleats, diamonds, squares, or a free-flowing design), the pattern must be sewn into the cover before the pieces are sewn together. With the design sewn into the upholstery material, the various pieces can be aligned (remember your notches or alignment marks) and sewn together. Remember to begin your seams at the center or alignment marks and to work outward from there.

Prior to sewing the seat cover together, think ahead and verify the order in which the pieces will be sewn together. No one method will be suitable for every seat. This is where a seasoned professional's experience makes a difference in the finished product.

Remember to sew the seat cover inside out. When all the pieces are sewn together, use a pair of shears to trim any excess material from the seams. Turn the cover right side out prior to installing it on the seat.

Three basic stitches used in automotive upholstery are the top stitch, the French seam, and the tuck and roll. No matter what stitch you use, make sure your stitches are straight. Nothing detracts from an upholstery job more than crooked stitches. Most trimmers use the presser foot of the sewing machine to align their stitches. Keep the foot's edge at the folded edge of your material and you won't have anything to worry about.

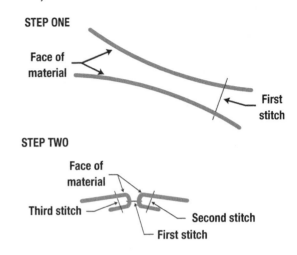

To sew a French seam, place two pieces of material face to face, with the common edge of both pieces aligned. Sew them together, with your sewing machine's presser foot running along their common edge. Fold both pieces of material over so that both faces are right side up. Sew a stitch through both layers of one piece of material with your second pass; then sew through both layers of the second piece of material with the third pass. Again, aligning the presser foot of your sewing machine with the edge of the material makes this process easy and consistent.

These two pieces of leather are sewn together using a French seam. They are part of a dash cover for a late-model Corvette and are meant to lie flat on a semirigid surface—so any excess material beneath the surface will be somewhat apparent. To minimize that effect, trim away excess material just outside the stitching. The width of the seam does not really matter as long as it's consistent. This type of attention to detail can make or break a trim job.

When sewing material together, also consider the length of the stitch. Most sewing machines let you adjust the number of stitches per inch. Eight stitches per inch yields stitches that are 1/8 inch long, four stitches per inch yields stitches that are 1/4 inch long, and so on. More stitches per inch provide a stronger seam; eight stitches is usually a reasonable number on the backside of material. For French seams or other topstitching, about 5 stitches per inch is right for automotive applications. If you prefer shorter stitches, six per inch is allowable. Four per inch is about the minimum.

STITCHES AND SEAMS

Topstitches

Topstitches are very common and provide a strong seam, with just one visible stitch. Place both pieces of material face to face and align the common edge. Attach the pieces by sewing about 1 inch. Lock the stitch by reversing the sewing machine to sew back to the beginning. Sew forward again, along the entire length of the material. At the end, reverse your sewing machine again and sew forward another inch to lock the stitch. Then fold one piece of material over so that both pieces are face-up. Sew through the two layers of the one piece of material and the single layer of the other piece of material.

This is an example of true pleats (more commonly known as tuck and roll). In this sample, stitch work began at the first pleat from the right. The fabric was folded face to face at this pleat and sewn to the foam. After being sewn the entire length, the material was pulled to the left and folded over face to face at the next pleat. No stitching is visible.

A topstitch can also be used to sew a pattern into a sewn panel, such as a seat cushion, seat back, or headliner. The pattern can simulate pleats (which should be parallel and consistent in width) or can be a freeform design of your choice. You simply sew stitches into a piece of material and the foam backing it is glued to. The thicker the foam, the more definition the pattern will have.

French Seams

A French seam is a great-looking stitch, but since the material lies flatter, the stitch is not necessarily stronger. Still, lots of patterns simply look better with a French seam. Rather than piping, which was popular in the 1950s and 1960s, French seams are a contemporary method of dressing up the connection between two pieces of material. When making a French seam, the two rows of side-by-side stitches must remain parallel and equidistant from one another. If you sew the way some people drive, your French seams will be a disaster.

Place both pieces of material face to face and align the common edge. Sew both pieces together by sewing about 1 inch. Lock the stitch by reversing your sewing machine and sewing back to the beginning. Move forward again, sewing the rest of the material. At the end, reverse your sewing machine and sew forward again for about 1 inch to lock the stitch. Fold both pieces of material over so that both pieces are face-up. Sew through the two layers of one piece of material for the entire length of the French seam. Then sew through the two layers of the remaining piece of material for the entire length of the French seam.

Tuck and Roll

Tuck and roll is not a stitch but rather a pattern, also known as true pleats. Many trimmers have not been taught the art and simply use a topstitch to simulate pleats. Back in the day, there was nothing quite like a "Tijuana tuck and roll"—at least as far as automotive upholstery was concerned. With a good tuck and roll, no stitching is visible.

Tuck and roll most likely got its name from tucking the material into the groove, sewing it in place, and then rolling the rest of the material over to the next groove. When sewing pleats, you are actually sewing material onto foam backing that will be slipped over the seat frame and cushion. Although it is getting more difficult to find, foam designed as a backing for tuck and roll upholstery has grooves cut into it at even spaces. Purchase foam with the appropriate thickness for the desired spacing between the pleats of your project. Do not fret if you cannot find pleated foam, as you can still sew pleats without it.

Prior to stitching, lay out the pleats on the material. Using a tape measure, mark the pleats at the top and bottom of the material, then connect the dots with a straightedge. For the first pleat, fold the material face to face at the first line and position the folded edge on the foam where the first stitch belongs. Pull the rest of the material over to the side you are starting from. (If you are working left to right, pull the excess material to the left; if you are working right to left, pull the excess material to the right.) Sew the material to the foam by sewing through the back of the excess and through the front of the short piece of material. When you finish sewing this stitch, roll the material over to the next pleat. Fold along the pleat line and sew the material to the foam by sewing through the back of the excess and through the front of the short piece of material. If you are doing this correctly, you should have one complete pleat and no visible stitches. Continue until the desired width is pleated.

INSTALLING THE NEW COVER

After all the pieces of the new seat cover are sewn with the design of your choice, it is time to slip the cover over the seat cushion or seat back. To allow the seat cover to slide into place more easily, most trimmers apply some talcum powder or "slickum" (a lubricating agent much like talcum powder) to the inside of the seat cover. You can find slickum or a reasonable alternative wherever upholstery materials and supplies are sold.

Gently slide the cover over the cushion to avoid ripping any material. Make sure the cover is properly aligned with the cushion and that all wrinkles are pressed out. When the cover is properly installed, it can be secured to the seat cushion or seat back. This is usually done by installing hog rings around a wire inserted through a listing (a wire, rod, or cord for the hog ring to hold on to) at the edges of the cover and around a wire or rod in the seat frame. Some newer seats have plastic clips that must be sewn to the lower edges of the cover and then hooked over the seat frame. It may be necessary to use a steamer to press out some wrinkles. Always verify that the cushion is aligned properly and is fully secured prior to steaming.

REINSTALLING THE SEAT

It takes only one person to install bucket seats, but a bench seat requires two people. While many people can pick up a bench seat easily enough, you'll need a second person to help you properly position it in the vehicle.

If the vehicle has studs that rise up from the floor, it is much easier to slide the seat mounting frames down over the studs. However, most seats are secured by threading a bolt into a weldment or threaded boss in the floor. If you stored the mounting bolts in their original mounting holes, remove them before positioning the seat. If floor covering or insulation covers the mounting holes, use an awl or ice pick to poke around to find the mounting holes. After finding one hole, set the seat into position, with the appropriate mounting holes aligned. Rotate the seat slightly in each direction to find the bolt hole for the kitty-corner mounting hole. With nonadjacent mounting holes aligned, the other two holes should automatically align.

At each mounting hole, use a razor knife to cut a small X or slit into the carpet. After you verify that the hole is indeed in the correct location, trim away enough carpet to fit the diameter of the bolt shaft. Push the mounting bolt through the seat's mounting surface and thread it into the insert or welded nut. On some custom vehicles, the seats may be secured with bolts that thread into nuts that are not welded to the underside of the floor pan. In this case, you'll need someone to hold a wrench on the nut from underneath the vehicle to secure the seat.

INSTALLING SEAT BELTS

While they are often overlooked by upholsterers, seat belts are an important part of any automobile's interior. New vehicle manufacturers are required to install seat belts, and most states require drivers and passengers to use them. Any number of reasons might lead you to install new seat belts in a vehicle. For instance, vehicles built before 1964 might not have seat belts at all. If they do have seat belts, older vehicles might not have three-point shoulder harness belts we are now accustomed to.

Seat belts are cheap and easy to install. If you are installing replacement seat belts into a vehicle that was originally equipped for them, simply bolt the ends of the new belts to the floor using the original hardware in the stock mounting locations. Then pass the latch ends up between the seat and back cushions of a bench seat or around the sides of bucket seats.

On the other hand, you may be installing seat belts for the first time on a street rod or other custom-built vehicle. Three-point shoulder harnesses are available from a number of suppliers at less than $100 per seat; lap belts are even less expense. For lap belts, you'll need to drill two holes in the floor pan, slightly behind the back of the seat cushions, leaving enough space to account for a wide variety of body types in the seats. On a bench seat, you can squeeze in a middle position if necessary. A three-point shoulder harness requires a third hole to be drilled in the B-pillar just behind the seat that the belt is intended for. To keep the bolts from pulling through the floor (or door pillar), use an anchor plate mounted beneath the floor pan to spread potential stress over a larger area.

PROJECT 2
Building Bucket Seats

 Time: 4–6 hours

 Skill Level: Medium

 Cost: Low

 Tools & Materials: MDF, wood glue, pencil, cordless drill, wood screws, L-brackets, compass, tape measure, angle-head sander (optional), straightedge, open-cell foam, electric carving knife, spray adhesive, table saw, scroll saw, circular saw, pneumatic stapler

This series of photos shows Sew Fine Interiors reupholstering a mid-1960s Plymouth Fury. Originally equipped with front bucket seats and a rear bench seat, the car will have four bucket seats and a full-length center console upon completion. At this point, sound dampening and thermal insulation have already been installed.

A base for the seats is fabricated out of MDF. After the seat base is fabricated, open-cell foam is glued together and shaped to form seat cushions. They can be covered with any desired material. Follow along as Brian Flynn fabricates the rear bucket seats to take the place of an original rear bench seat.

Constructing the seat base out of MDF is the first major step. The front crossmember is cut out to span the width of the vehicle and to fit the profile of the floor's structure (in this photo, the brown primer). Four more pieces are cut out to fit the floor pan. They are glued and screwed to the front crossmember and to two separate rear crossmembers. To tie the seat base together, a flat piece is glued and screwed between the left and rear seat and the front crossmember.

Simple L-shaped brackets and self-tapping sheet metal screws are used to secure the seat base to the floor pan. The brackets are located at each rear corner and each front corner of the seat base.

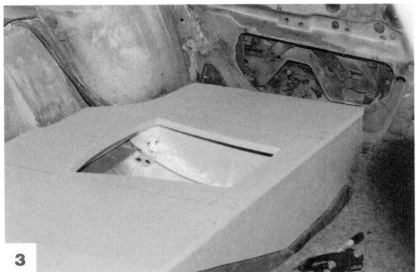

The top of the seat base is cut to fit flush along the front edge of the front crossmember and to conform to the outline of the body's sheet metal. The center leg of the compass can be moved along the sheet metal to trace the contour onto the MDF. The opening in the top allows for hidden storage under the seat cushion and is laid out using a template.

3

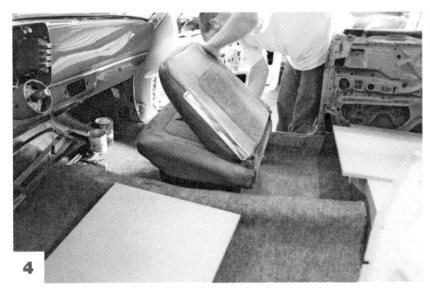

Secure one of the stock front seats in place to make sure back seat passengers will have adequate legroom. The stock front bucket seats will be reupholstered and reused for this project.

4

Add a second layer of MDF to the top of the seat base to place the new center console laterally. Take several measurements to properly locate the second layer of MDF. For this particular vehicle, the stock sheet metal seat back supports are not centered with the driveshaft tunnel. Never assume that anything from the factory is accurately centered or square.

5

After determining the correct location, use self-tapping screws to secure the second layer of MDF to the top of the seat base. This piece will eventually act as a spacer between the vertical portions of the center console.

Using the compass to draw an offset line from the interior body sheet metal, begin work on the seat cushion base of the rear passenger-side seat. The seat cushion must conform to the shape of the right rear wheelwell.

After cutting a piece of MDF for the wheelwell and rounding the front corners, check again for proper fit.

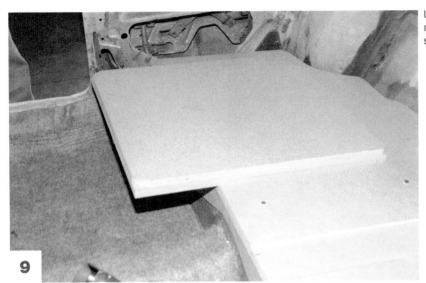

Using the same process as on the passenger side, mark and cut the seat cushion base for the driver-side seat.

9

The top of the seat base and each of the seat cushion bases are removed from the vehicle and spread out on a layout table. Bottom sides are up, so that the outline of the storage opening can be traced onto the bottoms of the seat cushion bases. Verify that the cushion bases are square with the seat base.

10

To assist in alignment of the cushion bases with the seat base, small blocks are cut and their edges rounded. The blocks are secured to the bottom of the seat cushion base with wood screws, allowing for a press fit of the seat cushion to ensure that it is properly repositioned when the storage area is utilized.

11

If necessary, use an angle-head sander to make sure the screw threads do not protrude through the seat cushion base and into the foam that will be applied.

Most seats are more comfortable if the front of the seat cushion is a bit taller than the back of the seat cushion. This is accomplished by adding extra foam to the front of the seat cushion to create a roll or bolster. Both seat cushion bases are aligned. A straight line represents the back edge of the added foam.

Select a piece of 1 1/2-inch-thick open-cell foam, mark a straight line, and cut a straight edge. The edge aligns with the line drawn in the previous photo.

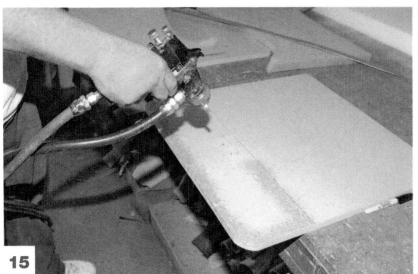

Apply spray adhesive to the seat cushion base from the line forward. More adhesive will be applied for the rest of the foam later, but right now we are concerned with the front bolster.

15

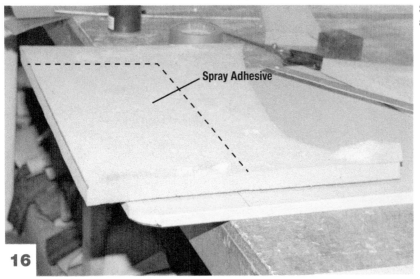

Spray adhesive is applied to the bottom of the foam as well.

Spray Adhesive

16

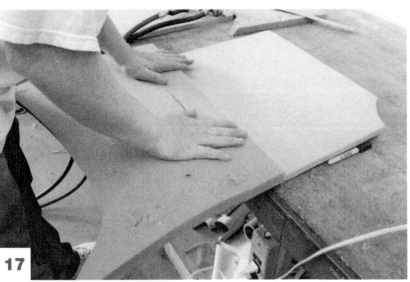

After the adhesive becomes tacky on both the seat cushion base and the foam, align the edge of the foam with the line on the base. Then press the foam down firmly.

17

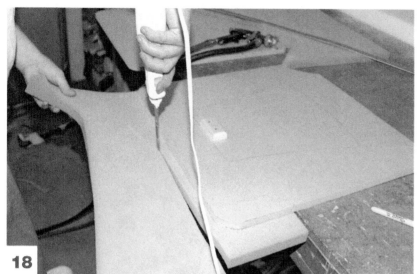

An electric carving knife is used to trim off excessive foam, eliminating the bulk of the excess. The foam does not have to be cut exactly at this point.

18

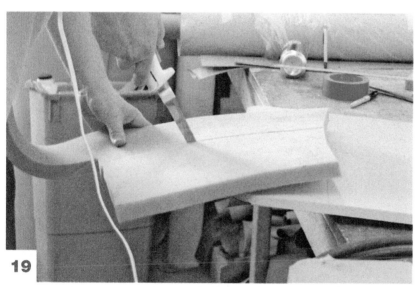

Cut out a piece of open-cell foam for the bolster for the second bucket seat. Multiple pieces of foam can be glued together, as long as there are no voids. Any voids or holes in the foam will show up when the customer begins sitting on the seats.

19

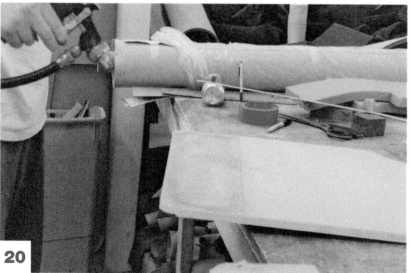

Apply spray adhesive to the front portion of the second seat cushion base. While it tacks up, cut two pieces of foam.

20

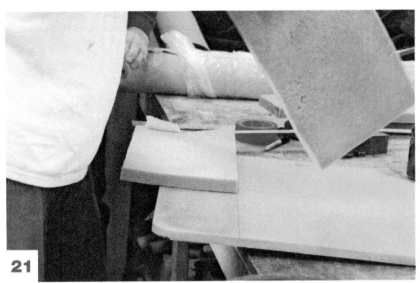

After spraying adhesive on both pieces of foam and allowing it to become tacky, align the edges of the foam with the line drawn on the seat cushion base. Make sure there is no gap between the pieces of foam.

The majority of the excess foam is cut off to get it out of the way. Another layer of foam will be added, and all the foam will be trimmed together more precisely.

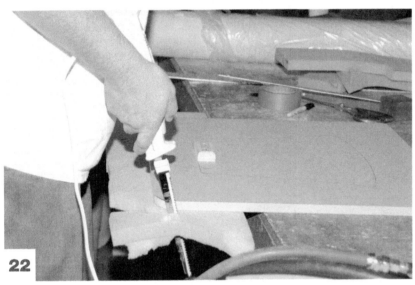

Set both seat cushion bases onto a piece of 3-inch open-cell foam to verify that it is large enough for both seats. After marking the size for each seat, cut out one piece of foam for each seat.

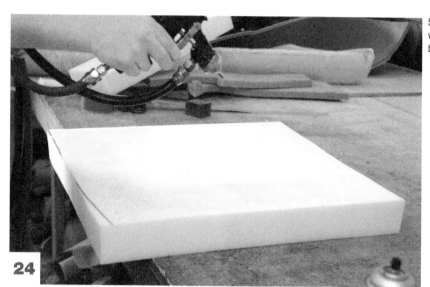

Spray adhesive must be applied to both surfaces for it to work correctly. Once again, apply spray adhesive on the bottom of the seat cushion foam.

Spray the top of the seat cushion base and the piece of foam that is already in place.

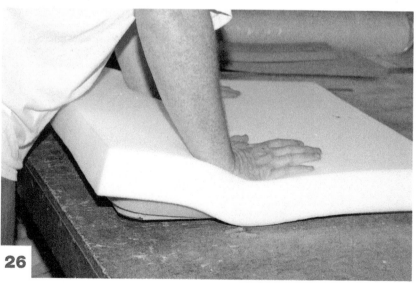

After the spray adhesive becomes tacky, position the open-cell foam onto the seat cushion base and press it into place. Press the entire piece of foam to verify that the two surfaces (seat cushion foam and seat cushion base) adhere to each other properly.

With the foam for the seat cushion in place, it is easy to see the difference that the extra foam across the front of the seat will make. With multiple layers of foam, the foam closest to the upholstery material or fabric should be the largest overall piece, so that the material lies flat and does not reveal a void in the foam.

27

With all the foam of the seat cushion in place, the excess foam can be removed with an electric carving knife.

28

With the seat cushions roughed in, set them in place to see how they look inside the vehicle. These cushions sit as Brian designed them, so he moves on to building the seat backs. Remember that a full-length console will take up the space between these bucket seats.

29

With a table saw and scroll saw, make the seat back out of MDF. After cutting it to conform to the shape of the body's interior sheet metal, cover the MDF with foam and eventually upholstery.

Each top corner of the seat back needs a radius, so grab something convenient to use as a template. In this case, a roll of painter's masking tape works just fine. Be sure to mark all corners at the same time (before more tape is used) so the arc templates are all the same.

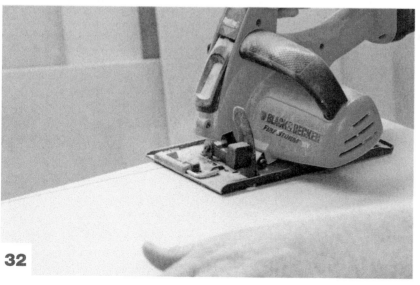

Using a circular saw, cut along the line that will be the taper in the shape of the seat back. This taper could be cut on a table saw, but a taper jig does it more properly.

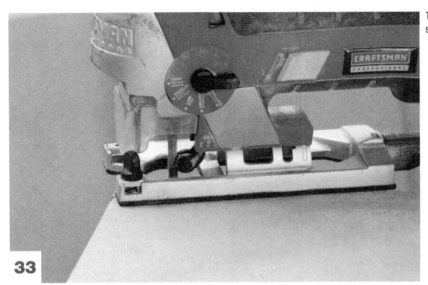

To cut the radius at the top of each seat back, use a scroll saw.

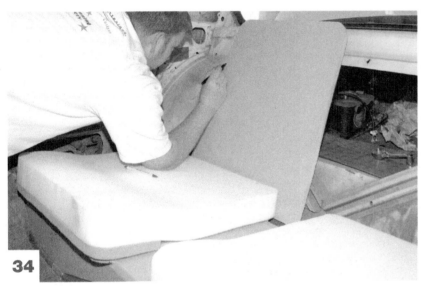

With the overall shape of the seat back cut, the piece of MDF is set in place in the vehicle. More cutting needs to be done, as the rear wheelwell encroaches into the seat back. Mark the area that needs to be trimmed away.

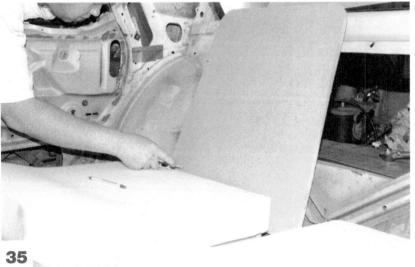

After sliding the seat back as close to the wheelwell as it will go, measure the offset between the seat back and the seat cushion. Set the compass to the same measurement, with a thickness allowance for the upholstery material. Instead of using the compass to draw a circle, slide the base of the compass along the wheelwell, marking the outline on the seat back at the same time.

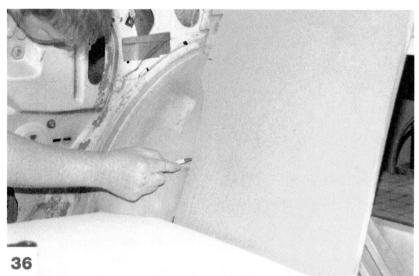

After being cut along the line, the seat back fits much better. Before adding any foam, check one last time for the proper fit.

36

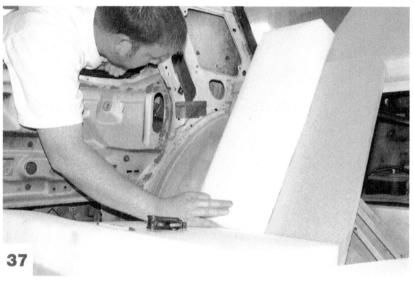

For the bulk of the seat back, more 3-inch open-cell foam is necessary. Bolsters will be added to the seat cushion and seat back.

37

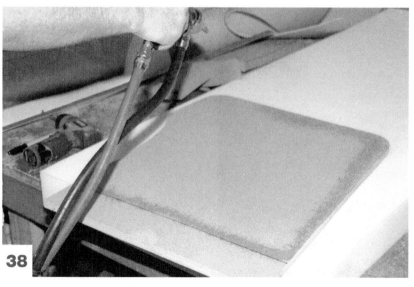

After drawing a line along the top of the seat cushion foam onto the seat back, you can see where the bottom edge of the seat back foam needs to be aligned. The area above that line is now sprayed with adhesive.

38

The 3-inch open-cell foam that will be used for the seat back is also sprayed with adhesive.

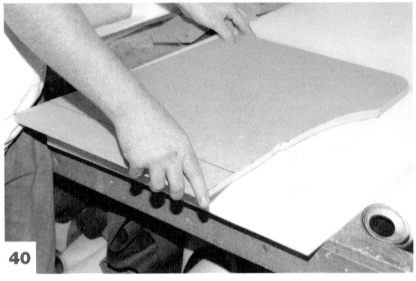

Looking at the back of the seat back, we now have a better idea of how much the right rear wheelwell encroaches on the back seat. When all is said and done, the rear passenger won't know any better. For now the seat back is placed face-down on the foam and aligned at the line that represents the top of the seat cushion foam.

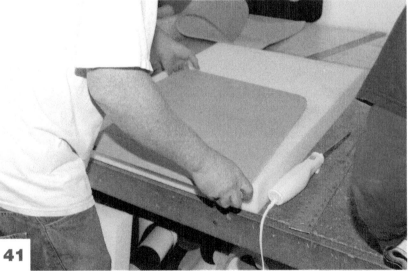

The same processes are followed for the driver-side rear seat back as well. Here the seat back is being positioned onto the foam.

Again, an electric carving knife is used to trim off the bulk of the excess foam. Bolsters will be created with more foam, so there is no need to be precise with trimming at this point.

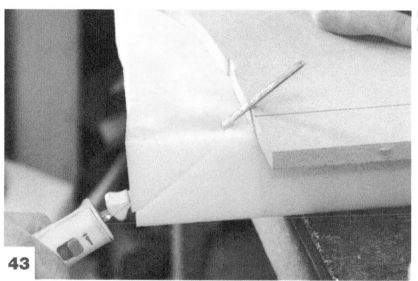

In the area of the wheelwells, the foam is cut at an angle, allowing it to fill the full width of the seat back.

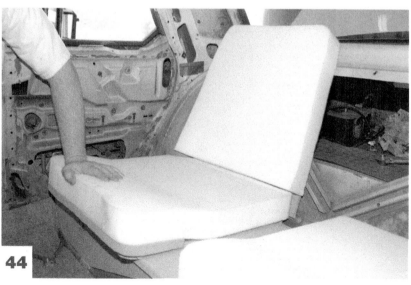

The complete bucket seat (less upholstery) is checked again. When fabricating anything, whether it is sheet metal, chassis structures, or seats, check your progress often to verify that you do not miss something critical.

The seat base can now be permanently attached to the substructure. Use a pneumatic stapler to secure the seat base to the front crossmember.

45

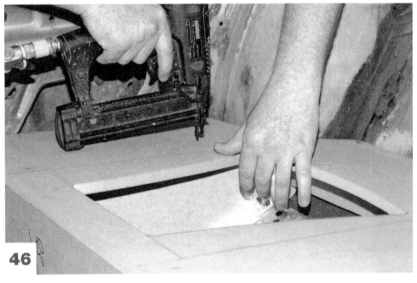

Also use a pneumatic staple gun to secure the seat base to the longitudinal portions of the substructure. Notice the predrawn template on the top of the seat base to indicate where the longitudinal portions are located.

46

Although they are not yet covered, it is easy to see how the rear bucket seats will look in their respective positions.

47

Brian has determined that side bolsters need to be added to the seat cushions. He has marked a line on each side of the cushion where the inner edge of the bolster will be placed.

48

Several pieces of open-cell foam need to be cut for the seat cushion and seat back bolsters. Mark the seat cushion and seat-back bolster patterns on a piece of foam. Each piece is the same width as the distance between the edge of the seat and the line in the previous photo. Use a carving knife to cut along the marked lines.

49

Since a rectangular bolster is uncomfortable and difficult to upholster, the inner top edge of each bolster is beveled. Cut a triangular section off the rectangular foam.

50

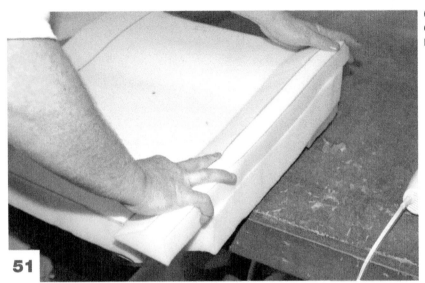

Check the bolsters for proper fit on the edge of a seat cushion. The bolsters will give the seat more style and will provide more lateral support to passengers.

Apply spray adhesive to the top of the seat cushion where the bolster will be attached.

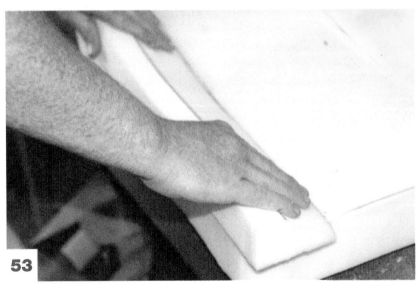

After applying spray adhesive to the bottom of the bolster and allowing both surfaces to become tacky, press the bolster into place.

Attach another bolster to the opposite side of the seat cushion. With spray adhesive, the foam can be pulled up and repositioned if necessary.

54

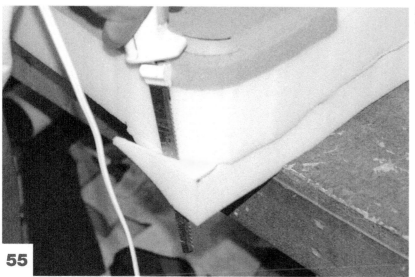

After flipping the seat cushion over, remove the excess foam of the bolster with a carving knife.

55

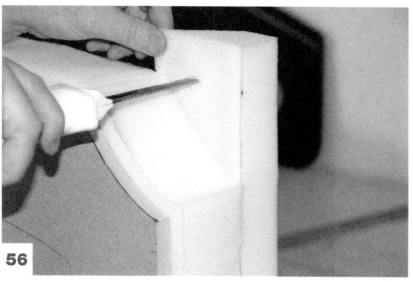

This is the bottom of the passenger-side seat cushion where the wheelwell encroaches. Remove the portion of the bolster that extends beyond the back of the seat cushion. The portion of the bolster above the wheelwell stays in place.

56

At the front of the seat cushion, bevel the bolster toward the front to provide a smooth contour.

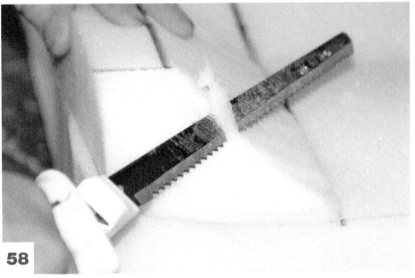

Continue to shape the foam with a carving knife. It is best to get the foam as close as possible to the final shape before any covering is installed.

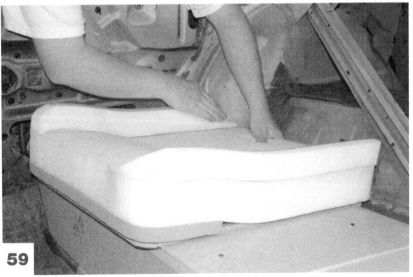

The seat cushions are shaping up quite nicely. When the seats are finished and covered, no one will know they are made of multiple pieces of foam.

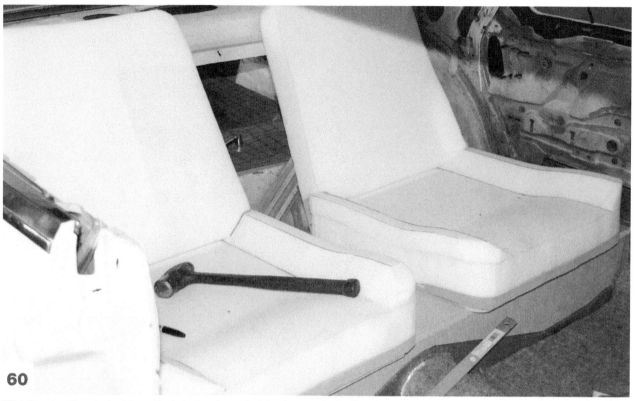

60

With both seat cushions glued and the seat backs in place, the rear bucket seats are coming together.

61

Bolsters on the seat cushions do not dictate that the seat backs must have them, but in this case, Brian feels that the seat backs should have bolsters. As with the seats, the backs of the bolsters are sprayed with glue.

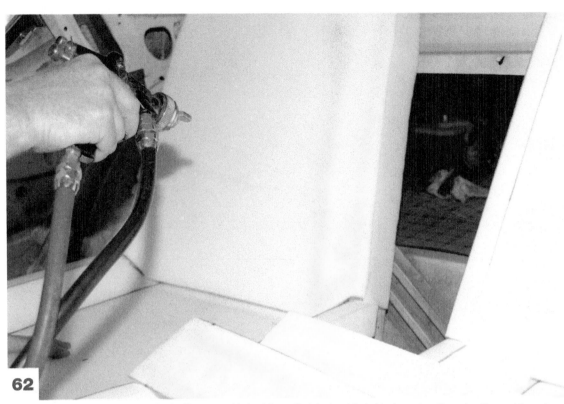

62 Also spray the seat back cushions with adhesive. You may need to do a bit more final shaping of the bolster foam where the seat cushions and the seat backs come together.

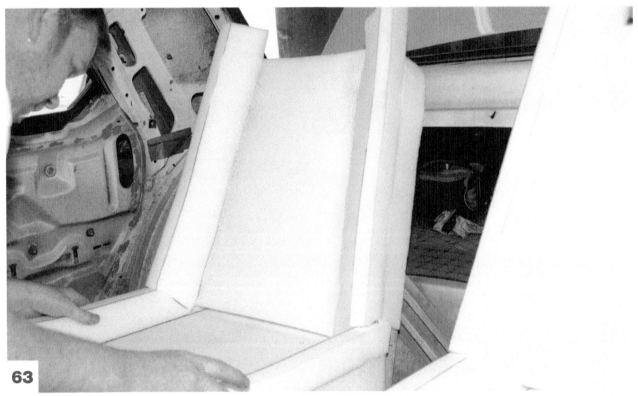

63 With the bolsters glued in place and the excess foam trimmed, the new rear bucket seats have been completely fabricated. To complete the project, sew together and install a seat cover.

PROJECT 3
Building and Covering a Vintage-Style Bench Seat

Time: 6+ hours

Skill Level: Medium–Advanced

Cost: Medium–High, depending on material

Tools & Materials: Electric drill, T-nut(s) and bolt(s), angle bracket(s), open-cell foam padding, adhesive spray, shears, razor blade, chalk, straightedge, sewing machine and thread, pneumatic stapler, silicone spray (optional), preferred cover material

Let's explore how a traditionally styled '33 Ford coupe hot rod is reupholstered with an aftermarket seat designed to emulate the original stock. The wooden framework is from LeBaron Bonney, with a metal framework from Keith Moritz, the owner of the car. The goal is to reupholster the aftermarket frame with an authentic tuck and roll trim job.

1

Looking much like the '33 Ford coupe original, this seat is all new thanks to the aftermarket wooden frame. The custom metal framework allows the seat to be moved forward or backward to suit the driver.

2

With the wooden seat frame in position, drill a hole through it and the underlying metal framework near each front corner. Install a T-nut in the seat frame, allowing a bolt to be inserted through the metal framework and into the seat frame, securing both in place.

3

Drill a hole through the wooden seat back framework and the plywood seat back, allowing a T-nut to be inserted into the plywood seat back. Insert a bolt through the wooden seat back framework and into the plywood seat back, securing the latter in place after it is upholstered. T-nuts let you install a threaded insert into a piece of wood, allowing the assembly to be bolted together after the panels are upholstered.

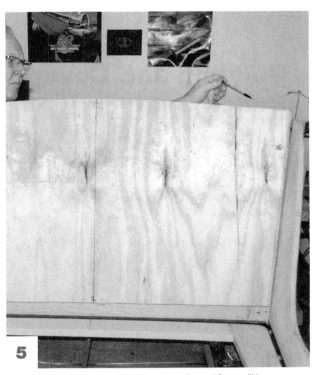

4

The hex head bolt toward the top passes through the wooden seat back framework and threads into the T-nut in the plywood seat back. Use an angle bracket to secure the side panel to the wooden seat back framework.

5

The plywood seat back, two side panels, and wooden seat frame will be reupholstered when the job is done. The side panels will simply be covered with foam and vinyl, with no pattern. The seat cushion and seat back will be done in a traditional tuck and roll.

6

Now that the entire seat has been fastened together, it can be taken apart and the upholstery process can begin.

7

Each side panel needs a piece of 1/4-inch open-cell foam glued on each side (four total). The foam will be covered by a black vinyl cover comprised of two similarly shaped pieces of vinyl sewn together. Here, the first piece of foam to be cut is marked.

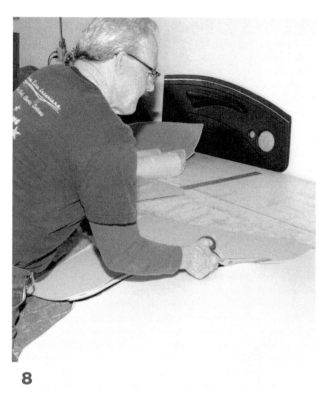

8

After cutting the first piece of foam, flip it over and use it as a pattern for the next piece. Repeat for the next pair.

9

Apply spray adhesive to the back of one piece of foam and to the corresponding side of the panel.

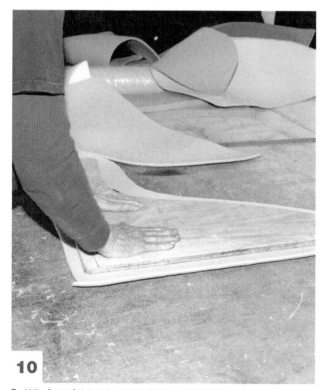

10

To rid the foam of air bubbles, place it flat on a layout table and place the plywood side panel onto it. Press the plywood to make sure it makes good contact with the foam.

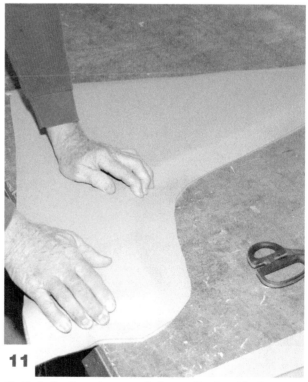

11

After flipping the side panel over, press the foam over the edges of the plywood.

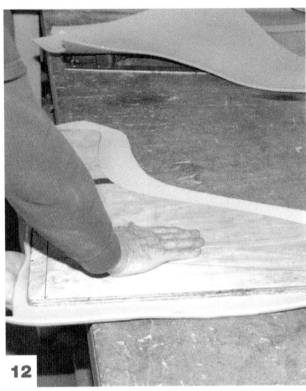

12

Use a razor blade beneath the plywood to cut excess foam from the straight edges of the plywood.

13

The curved portions of the side panel will be a little tricky. Continue to apply spray adhesive to the back of the exposed foam and to the edges of the plywood.

14

Slits cut into the foam allow it to expand and contract to match the edge of the plywood. Any extra foam is removed with a razor knife.

15

One side of the first piece of plywood has been covered in foam. The other side remains to be covered. Apply spray adhesive to the exposed plywood and the corresponding piece of foam.

16

Press the plywood onto the foam, verifying that firm contact is made over the entire piece.

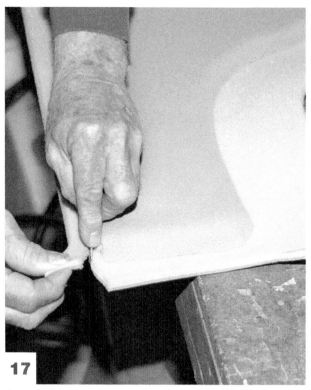

17

Use a razor blade to cut off the excess foam. Since one side of the foam is wrapped around the edge of the plywood, the other side will cover the face of one of the bench seats. Repeat the previous steps for the second side panel.

18

Now it's time to cover the side panels. The first step is to create piping to cover the edge. Mark two 1 1/2-inch-wide strips on black vinyl material.

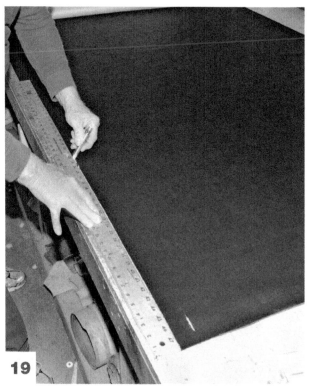

19

Using a long straightedge and chalk, mark cut lines on the black vinyl, and cut the dual strips of vinyl with shears.

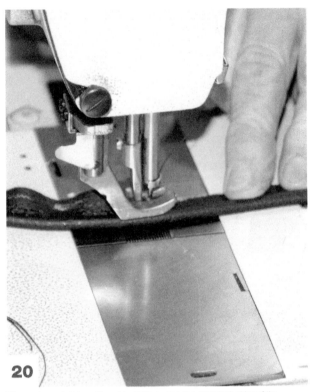

20

Wrap a piece of piping with a strip of black vinyl and stitch both sides of the material together. The material should be stitched as close to the piping as possible. Each piece of side panel material will be sewn to the two remaining flaps.

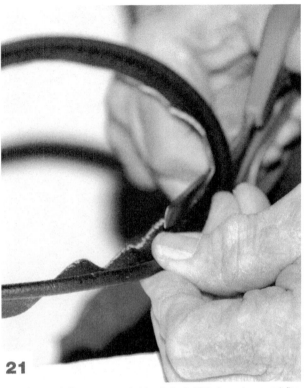

21

Using shears, cut off any excess material so that only 1/4 inch remains on each flap. This will eliminate a buildup of excess material under the narrow edge.

22

Use chalk to mark an outline on the black vinyl material around the curved portion of the foam-covered side panel.

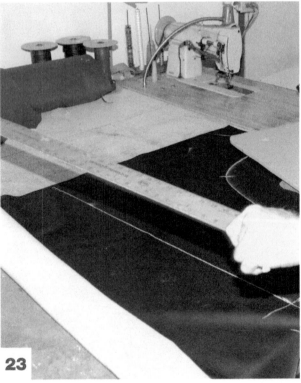

23

Use a straightedge to mark the straight sides of the side panel onto the vinyl.

24

After the first piece of vinyl is cut, place it face-down on another piece of vinyl and mark the outline with chalk.

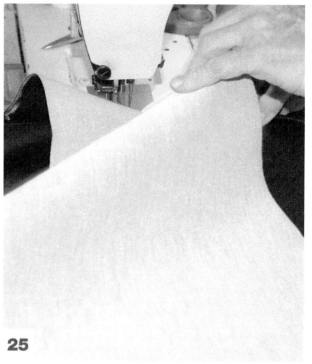

25

To sew the cover together, fold over approximately 1/4 inch of the side panel cover material so that the face of the cover material and the face of the piping are facing each other. Verify that the piping is aligned with the correct starting spot on the cover. Sew approximately 1 inch. Reverse the sewing machine and sew back to the beginning to lock the stitch. Continue sewing the piping to the first side cover.

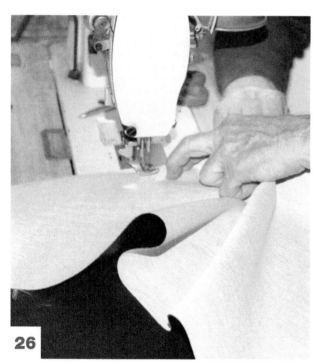

26

Repeat the process to secure the second piece of side cover material to the first, which now has piping along the mutual edge. Do not sew along the bottom edge, as this cover must be slid over the padded side panel. With the bulk of your sewing, the back of the material faces up.

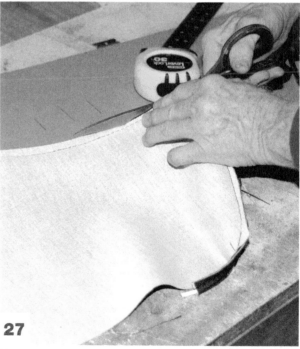

27

With both pieces of side panel material sewn together and the piping installed, any excess can be trimmed from the back.

28

The white spots on the foam are access holes for the T-nuts, so the seat can be reassembled. Mark these locations on the lower edge of the side panel, so the T-nuts will be easier to find after the cover is installed.

29

To make installing the side cover a bit easier, spray a light coating of silicone spray onto the foam padding of the side panel. The bottom and back edges will not be sewn. Nonetheless, material that slides easily makes for a better installation.

30

Pull the cover into position and verify that the piping is centered along the top edge of the plywood. When the curved edge is in position, pull the bottom outside material up and over the bottom edge of the plywood.

31

Use a pneumatic stapler to attach the outer material to the inside of the plywood. Having extra material gives you more leverage as you pull the material tight. After it is stapled in place, carefully remove excess material with a razor blade.

24

After the first piece of vinyl is cut, place it face-down on another piece of vinyl and mark the outline with chalk.

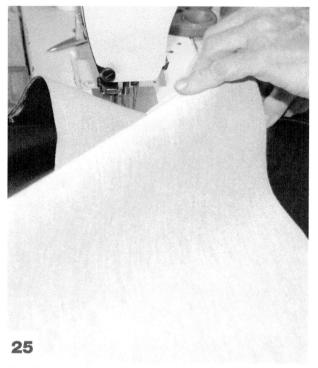

25

To sew the cover together, fold over approximately 1/4 inch of the side panel cover material so that the face of the cover material and the face of the piping are facing each other. Verify that the piping is aligned with the correct starting spot on the cover. Sew approximately 1 inch. Reverse the sewing machine and sew back to the beginning to lock the stitch. Continue sewing the piping to the first side cover.

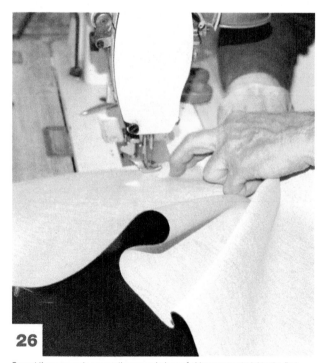

26

Repeat the process to secure the second piece of side cover material to the first, which now has piping along the mutual edge. Do not sew along the bottom edge, as this cover must be slid over the padded side panel. With the bulk of your sewing, the back of the material faces up.

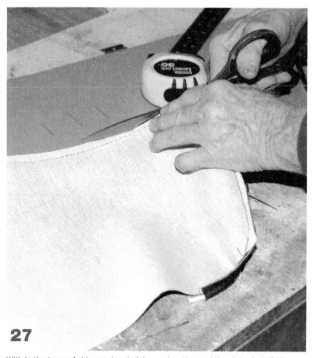

27

With both pieces of side panel material sewn together and the piping installed, any excess can be trimmed from the back.

28

The white spots on the foam are access holes for the T-nuts, so the seat can be reassembled. Mark these locations on the lower edge of the side panel, so the T-nuts will be easier to find after the cover is installed.

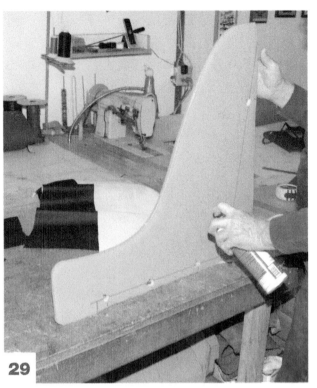

29

To make installing the side cover a bit easier, spray a light coating of silicone spray onto the foam padding of the side panel. The bottom and back edges will not be sewn. Nonetheless, material that slides easily makes for a better installation.

30

Pull the cover into position and verify that the piping is centered along the top edge of the plywood. When the curved edge is in position, pull the bottom outside material up and over the bottom edge of the plywood.

31

Use a pneumatic stapler to attach the outer material to the inside of the plywood. Having extra material gives you more leverage as you pull the material tight. After it is stapled in place, carefully remove excess material with a razor blade.

32 Pull the outside material around the back edge of the plywood and staple it in place. Make sure you pull the material tight before you staple it.

33 Use a razor blade to trim off the excess material. The inside panel will cover the overlap from the lower and back edges, but avoid excessive material, as its edges will telegraph outward if it's in the middle of a panel.

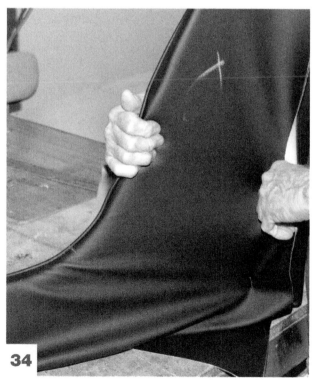

34 Pull the inside panel into position. Make sure the piping stays in place along the center of the edge of the plywood.

35 Staple the inside panel along the same line the outside panel was stapled on so that the seat back cushion hides the staples. When the finished seat is in the vehicle, it is unlikely anyone will see the staples, but still try to hide all staples and fasteners.

36

Trim the excess from the back edge with a razor blade. Repeat all previous steps for the opposite side panel.

37

With both side panels covered, carefully probe the upholstery and foam to locate the T-nuts beneath them. Once you've found the T-nuts, bolt the side panels to the metal framework. When the seat is completely finished, these bolts will be hidden by the seat cushion.

SEATING

38

These two angle brackets and the rest of the seat back will be visible when the seat is completed, but will not be seen after the seat is installed in the vehicle.

39

Bar Clamp

The seat cushion and seat back could be covered in the same method as the side panels, but that wouldn't be very comfortable. To prevent the seat from moving around, use a bar clamp (at the front center of the seat) to temporarily secure it to the table.

40

For an old-fashioned seat, old-fashioned methods (in this case, stapling) are sometimes best. Since the wooden seat frame is simply a perimeter piece, attach 3-inch-wide webbing to the frame with staples. Use two strips of webbing on the lateral sides. Use several staples to attach the webbing so that you don't have to replace it later if it snaps.

41

Determine how many strips of seat webbing are required to fill the seat from side to side, and make the appropriate marks on the wooden seat frame. Staple one end of the seat webbing in place, weave it through the lateral webbing, pull it taut, and then staple it to the frame.

42

Use several staples to secure the seat webbing and a razor blade or utility knife to cut the webbing material. Cut the webbing material so that it ends about 1/2 inch from the edge of the wooden seat frame.

43

Pull the seat webbing as tight as humanly possible, as the material stretches with use. The webbing ultimately supports the weight of the driver and passenger, so it is not going to get any firmer with age.

44

For the driver and passenger to recline a tad, the seat back foam needs to be 4 inches thick at the bottom and 3 inches thick at the top. To get the most out of the open-cell foam, mark alternating measurements of 3 inches and 4 inches across the top, and alternating measurements of 4 inches and 3 inches across the bottom.

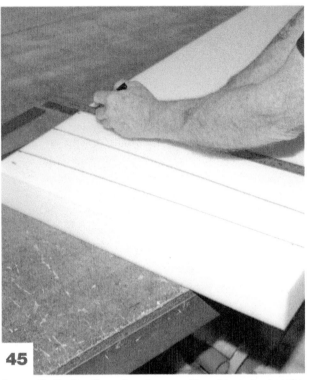

45

By connecting the alternating marks on the open-cell foam, it is easy to cut a series of tapered pieces of foam.

46

While a foam saw or carving knife could be used to cut the foam, a band saw is used instead. The band saw is notably quicker, and it sure won't hurt the foam.

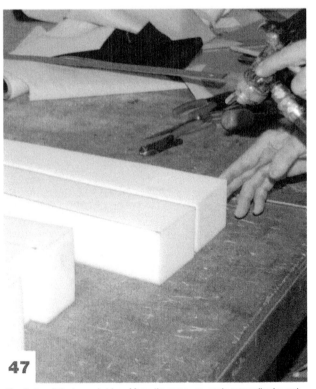

47

After facing all the tapered strips of foam the same way, apply spray adhesive and glue them together.

48
After several pieces of foam are glued and pressed together, the end shape is a wedge that is 3 inches thick at the top, 4 inches thick at the bottom, and wide enough to span the seat back.

49
Scuff the plywood with a sanding block so that the spray adhesive sticks better. Anything between 50- and 120-grit sandpaper works well for this. You don't want to gouge the plywood; you simply want to rough it up a bit to increase adhesion of the glue.

50
Spray both the back of the wedge of open-cell foam and the face of the seat back plywood with adhesive (apply a heavy coat, as the seat back will be subject to a fair amount of wear). If the seat back cushion begins moving around on the plywood, the quality of the upholstery work will quickly diminish.

51
After the adhesive becomes tacky, place the plywood onto the foam and press it into place.

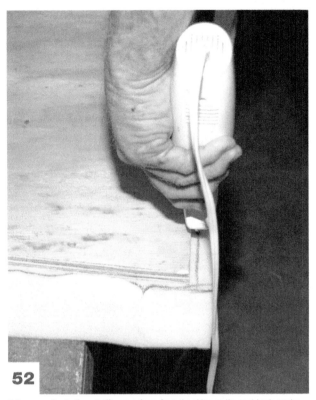

52

Using a carving knife, cut off excess foam from the sides, so the seat back can be set into position.

53

The seat back cushion needs to be trimmed across the top to match the curve of the plywood seat back.

54

After trimming the top of the foam to match the plywood, set the seat back into position.

55

Measure to find the center of the seat's width. Mark a centerline perpendicular to the seat base.

56

Repeat the previous steps (measuring, marking, cutting the foam, and gluing the pieces together) for the seat cushion.

57

With both cushions (seat and seat back) glued together and trimmed to the correct shape, the uncovered seat back is revealed. The dark lines on the cushions show where the pleats will be, although nothing further will be done to the foam.

58

This seat has six 5-inch-wide pleats in the middle, with the balance of the width taken up by the remaining material. Sew the cover of the seat cushion first, and begin the layout on the 1/2-inch open-cell foam by marking the 5-inch wide pleats.

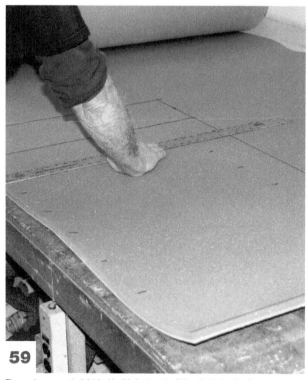

59

The seat cover material (vinyl in this instance) will be stitched to the foam at each of the pleats. Mark a line on the foam where each pleat is to be sewn.

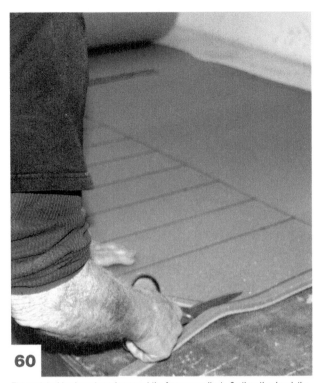

60

The seat cushion is rectangular, so cut the foam accordingly. On the other hand, the seat back is tapered on the end to match the slope of the side panels. Be aware of such subtle details when you cut, so you do not create excessive waste.

61

This foam for the seat cushion shows exactly where the pleats will be. The top of the seat cushion will be pleated, while the front panel of the seat cushion will be covered by a flat piece of vinyl.

62

With the foam cut for the seat cover, turn your attention to the foam for the seat back cover. As with the seat cushion cover, cut it slightly larger than necessary and trim it to the correct size later.

63

The same 5-inch-wide pleats are marked on the foam to match the seat cushion. Unlike on the seat cushion, the pleats wrap over the top of the seat back cushion. Remember that the sides of the seat back will be angled to match the slope of the side panels.

64

Beginning with the vinyl for the seat cushion, lay out the overall size of the cover. Begin by laying out the front-to-back measurement. Mark it with chalk, which can easily be wiped off the vinyl later.

65

Use chalk and a metal straightedge to connect the dots and get a line showing the back of the seat cushion. The finished pleats will be 5 inches wide and are marked that way on the foam. The outer material (the vinyl) must be marked at 5 1/2 inches to allow for the tuck before the roll.

66

The pleats must be parallel with each other and perpendicular to the front and rear edges of the seat cushion. Use a carpenter's framing square to ensure they are laid out correctly.

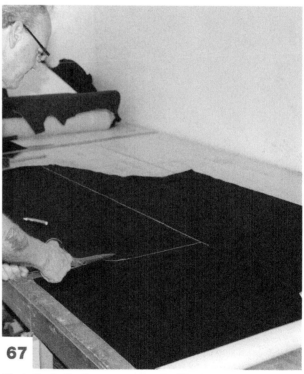

67

After double-checking the measurements and verifying the layout, cut the vinyl for the seat cushion.

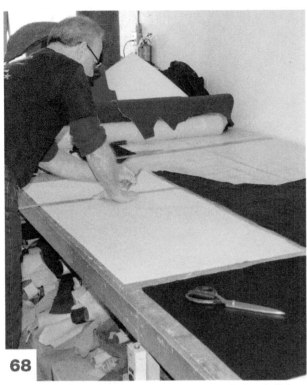

68

Mark the pleats on the back of the vinyl so that it can be properly aligned with the foam once it is sewn.

69

After repeating the layout and cutting the vinyl for the seat back cover, lay out the pleats on the back of this material as well.

70

Finally, connect the dots to actually lay out the pleats. Remember that the spacing on the vinyl is 1/2 inch wider than the marks on the foam to allow for the tuck and roll. Lay out the pleats for the seat cushion and seat back at the same time before moving on to the next step, sewing the foam and vinyl together.

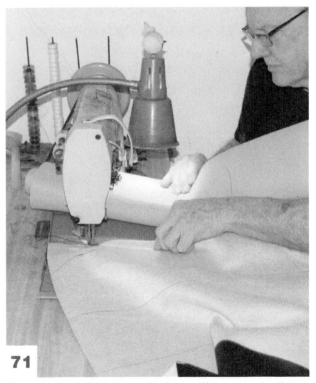

71

When sewing true pleats, start on one side of the panel being sewn and continue across it. Whether you work left to right or right to left is up to you. Regardless, be prepared for a significant amount of material rolled up under your sewing machine.

72

As you sew the first of the true pleats, note that the foam (blue) and everything except the first section of the vinyl upholstery is face side up. Stitch through both layers of the same piece of vinyl material and through the foam.

73

Here we can see a little more clearly the blue foam material, the black face of the vinyl material sewn to it, and the gray backing of the vinyl material. After you finish stitching this pleat, unfold the unsewn material over to the next pleat and align and sew the next two lines.

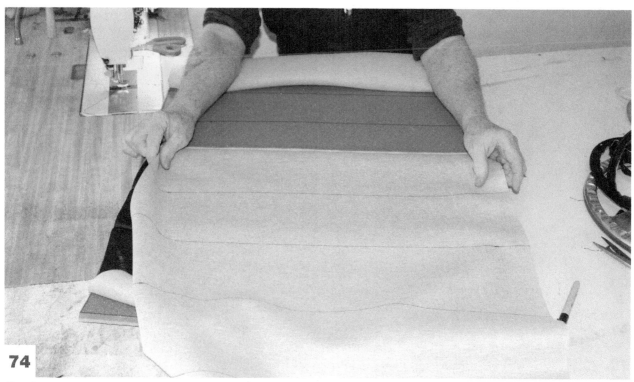

74

After a few pleats, the tuck and roll is coming along nicely. It doesn't matter which way you work, as long as you're consistent. A few more stitches and the seat cushion cover will be finished.

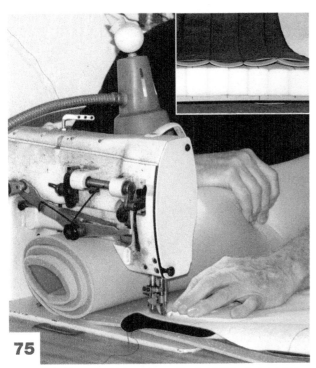

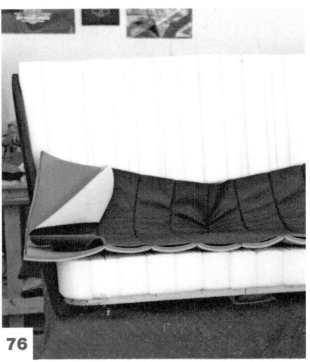

75

The foam is laid face-up under the sewing machine foot. With the vinyl material face down on the foam, the dual pleat lines aligned, and the rest of the vinyl folded over, the vinyl is stitched through both layers. The inset shows the wooden base of the seat, the foam seat cushion, and the 1/2-inch open-cell foam, which will ultimately be covered by the tuck and roll vinyl seat cover. The true beauty of tuck and roll is that no stitching is visible.

76

Once the tuck and roll portion of the seat cushion cover is complete, trim it to the correct size to fit the top of the seat cushion. Cut another panel of vinyl material, add piping, and sew the panel to the sides and front of the seat cushion cover. The seat back cushion is covered in similar fashion, with a second piece of vinyl covering the back and sides, with piping at the seam.

77

Voila! A brand-new vintage-style seat with old-fashioned tuck and roll upholstery is ready to be installed in the 1933 Ford coupe. The lever in the lower right portion of the photo controls the slide mechanism, allowing the seat to move forward or backward after being installed.

SEATING

PROJECT 4
Repairing or Replacing a Panel on a Seat

Time: 2–4 hours

Skill Level: Easy

Cost: Low

Tools & Materials: Hog ring pliers, single-edged razor blade or utility knife, listing, shears, sewing machine, chalk or china marker, cordless drill & bits (variable), preferred upholstery material

While the bulk of your upholstery experience might be gained from complete vehicle upholstery jobs, a small portion will undoubtedly involve making repairs. You might have to replace a panel of a torn or burned seat cover or remove adjustable headrests that the customer no longer wants. When Jerry Klitch at Sew Fine Interiors recovered these seats, he suggested that the adjustable headrests be removed. After the upholstery job was completed, the customer realized that Jerry's idea was indeed a good one and brought them back for removal.

The process of replacing the panel of the seat cover where the headrest slides in and out also shows how to remove a seat cover to use it as a pattern for a new cover. You will save a considerable amount of time during your upholstery career if you learn to use existing covers as patterns.

1

Jerry is going to be working only on the seat back cushions of a pair of bucket seats, so they have been removed from the seat cushion.

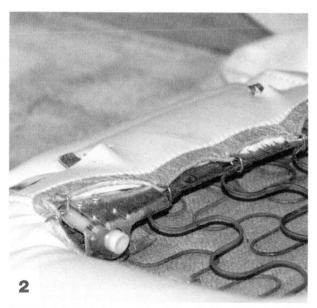

2

The adjustable headrests slide up and down in the white tubes near the top of the seat backs. These need to be removed. The upholstered panel that the headrest slides through needs to be replaced.

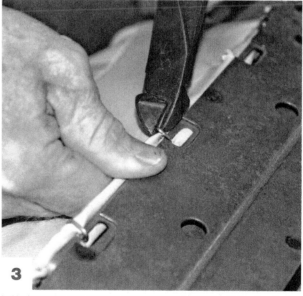

3

In this vintage seat, seat covers are secured to the seat assembly with hog ring pliers. Using a pair of diagonal (side) cutters and a twisting motion, remove the hog rings.

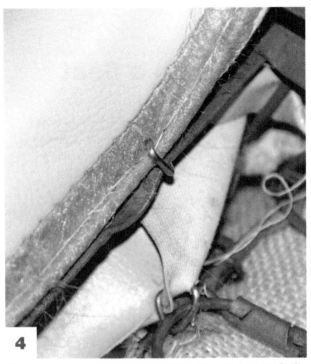

4

When hog rings are used to secure a seat cover, wire, rod, or cord, listing (usually 1/8 inch in diameter or smaller) is sewn to the edges of the cover. The listing provides something stronger than the upholstery material for the hog ring to grab hold of. The listing here is made much like piping (a strip of material wrapped around the cord or piping material is sewn closed and then sewn to the surrounding material).

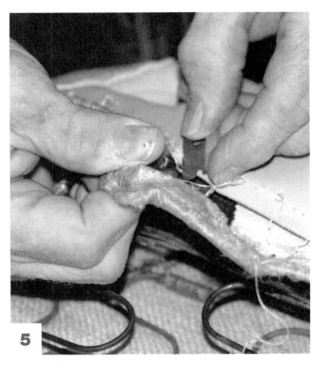

5

In this area, the listing can be reused, but it must first be removed from the seat cover. Use a single-edge razor blade to carefully cut the necessary stitches.

6

After making the first few cuts, pull the listing away gently, making the stitches easier to cut.

7

In this particular situation, the top panel and the side panels are separate pieces of material, allowing for an easy repair. Still, the top panel must be separated from the side panels. The stitches that hold them together need to be cut. There are many, but it is still less time-consuming than making an entirely new seat cover.

SEATING

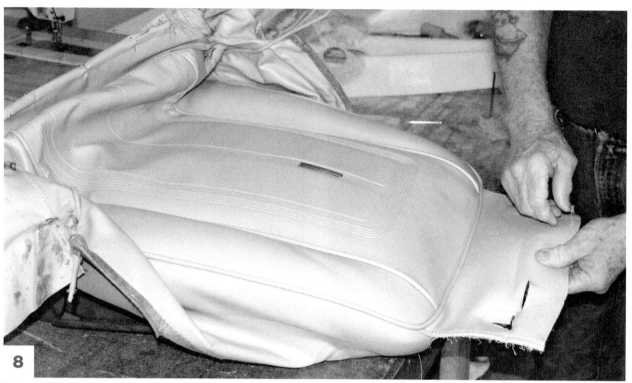

8 The top panel in hand is going to be replaced. Other than the unsightly slits for the headrest, nothing else was wrong with the seat cover. This is a simple and relatively easy repair.

9 As more stitches are cut, it becomes easier to pull the connected panels apart, making it easier to cut the remaining stitches. Make sure you do not cut any material that is to be reused.

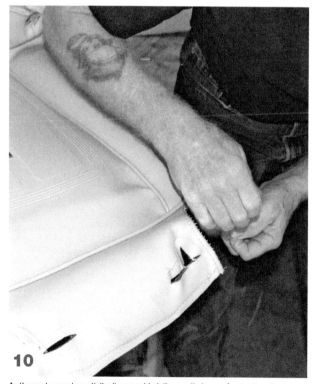

10 As the seat cover is partially disassembled, the small pieces of sewn-together material become obvious. Old covers can be disassembled and used to make patterns for new covers.

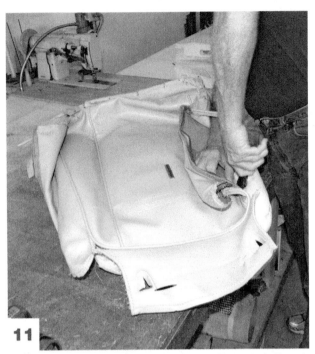

11 This particular seat and many others utilizes various sets of listings to give the seat its overall shape. The majority of the seat back is one piece of material. A narrower piece of material covers the inside of each side bolster, while another piece covers each of the outer sides of the bolsters.

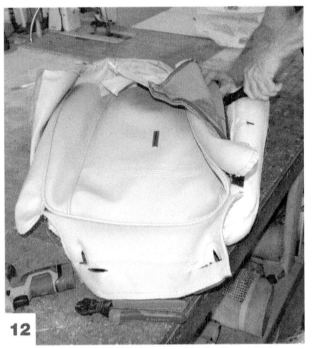

12 To maintain the shape of the seat cover, an inner listing surrounds the big panel in the middle of the seat back cushion while an outer listing is located near the back edge. The hog rings securing the middle back panel must be installed first but removed last. The outer hog rings must be removed first but would have been installed last.

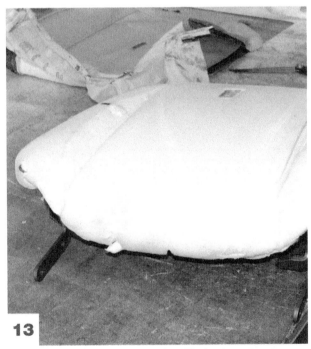

13 The unskinned seat cushion back is shown here. This view shows why an inner listing is used to secure the middle panel of the cover and an outer listing is used to secure the outer portions of the cover to the back of the seat back cushion. If the inner listing were not used, the cover would stretch across the high points, eliminating the contour of the cushion beneath.

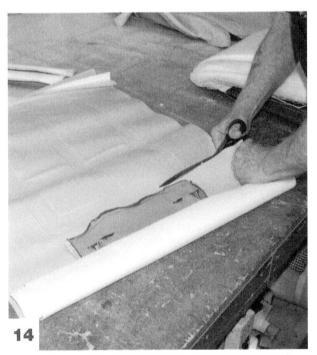

14 Factory replacement seat cover material, complete with an embossed pattern for this particular vehicle, was available, so Jerry used that to match the previous upholstery. The next step is to cut a piece of replacement material large enough for the new panel.

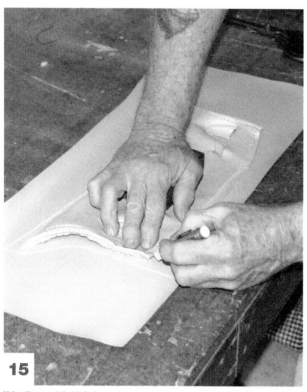

15

Using the panel that is being replaced as a pattern, mark around it with a piece of chalk and cut out the pattern with a pair of shears.

16

An existing piece of upholstery was used as a pattern, so the material can be cut out on the line. There is no need for any extra material.

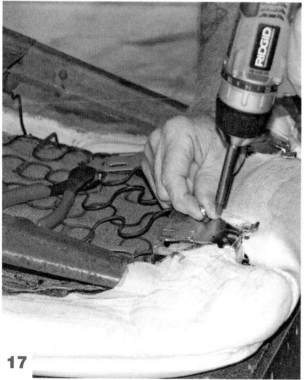

17

Since the adjustable headrests have been removed, the ratcheting mechanism in the seat back can be removed as well.

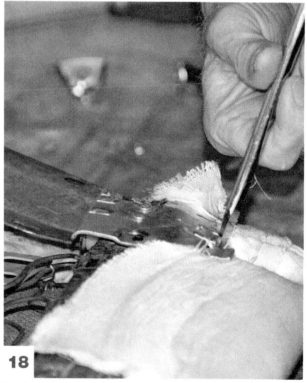

18

Securing mechanisms vary from one vehicle to another, so each vehicle broadens your knowledge base. On this vehicle, both hex head bolts and slotted screws were used, making a variety of nonupholstery tools a necessity.

19

Now that the new panel has been cut from new material, all that is left to do is sew it back in place.

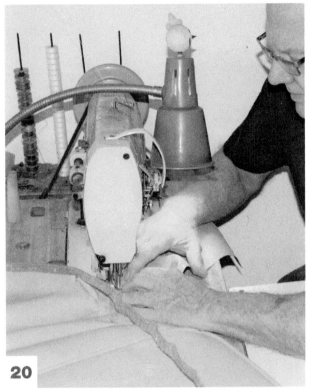

20

Align the replacement top panel and the middle panel of the seat back and sew them together.

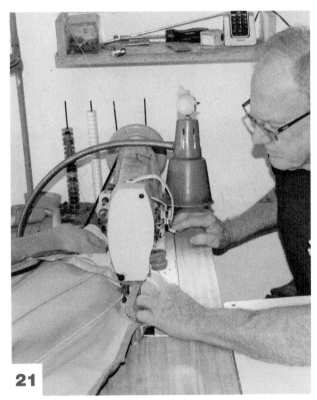

21

Sew the new top panel to each of the side panels.

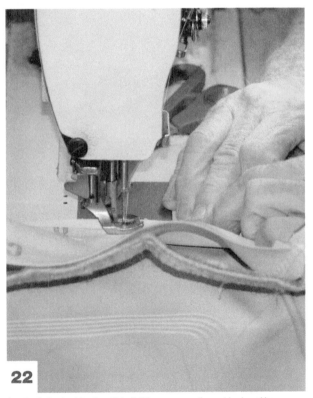

22

Sew the listing back in place. Reinstall the cover over the seat back cushion, reconnect that to the seat cushion, and reinstall the seats into the vehicle.

PROJECT 5
Covering a Bucket Seat

Time: 4–6 hours

Skill Level: Medium

Cost: Medium

Tools & Materials: China marker, shears, open-cell foam padding, adhesive spray, hog rings, listing, hog ring pliers, contact cement, sewing machine and thread, J-clips, screwdriver, ratchet, wrench, preferred cover material

Longtime upholsterer Don Albers is still practicing his craft, but now he has an apprentice. Nick Mayden is a graduate of WyoTech (Pennsylvania) and appears to have been paying attention in class. Nick and Don were covering

seats for a 1932 Ford Tudor street rod and allowed me to take some photos. Follow along as they show one way to cover a pair of traditional bucket seats. A bench seat could be covered using the same basic procedure.

1 Cut out patterns for all the pieces required to cover the seat and lay them on the material to be cut. Arrange the patterns to make the best use of the material. You can get by with one pattern for pieces of the same shape, but remember how the pattern needs to be oriented, so you don't end up with two left flaps and none for the right.

2 Use lead weights to hold the pattern flush with the material and trace around it with a white china marker. China markers work best on vinyl or leather; chalk works best on cloth or tweed.

3 With all the pieces lying flat and marked on the material, use a pair of upholstery shears to cut them out. Cut the pieces slightly bigger than the pattern. Be careful not to cut into adjacent pieces.

4

Place the oversize pieces of vinyl on the open-cell foam that will pad the material. Place the pieces so that the minimal amount of material (foam in this case) is used.

5

Each piece of vinyl needs to be glued to the foam. Fold each piece of vinyl over on itself. Spray the back of the vinyl and the front of the foam with contact cement. After the glue becomes tacky, press the vinyl into place, smoothing out any wrinkles or bubbles. Fold the opposite side of vinyl over, apply contact cement to the remaining vinyl and foam, and repeat.

6

With all the vinyl pieces glued to the foam, again cut out each individual piece. At this point, each piece should still be oversize.

7

To keep the vinyl material and the foam attached, stitch around the perimeter of each piece of vinyl.

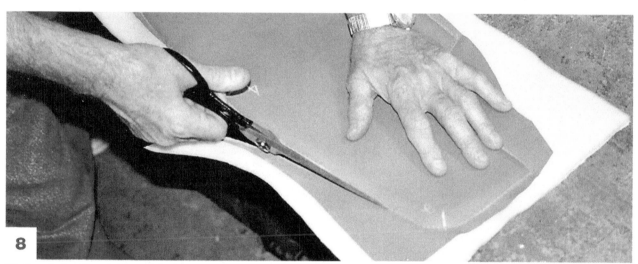

8

With the perimeter of the material sewn to the foam, cut each piece of vinyl to its actual size. Be sure you don't cut inside the stitching.

9

A close look at this piece of vinyl reveals numbered reference marks. These will be used to properly align this piece with the pieces it attaches to.

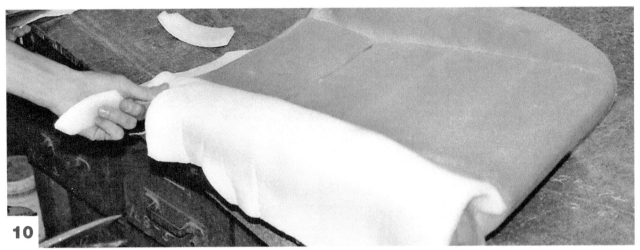

10

The seats being re-covered are molded foam and show some signs of wear. To smooth up the bolsters and to provide some additional cushion, cut a piece of open-cell foam to fit on the inside and outside of the seat's side bolsters.

11

Apply contact cement to both the outside of the molded foam seat cushion and the back of the foam that covers it. Allow the adhesive to become tacky and then press it into position. Carefully trim off any excess foam material with a pair of upholstery shears.

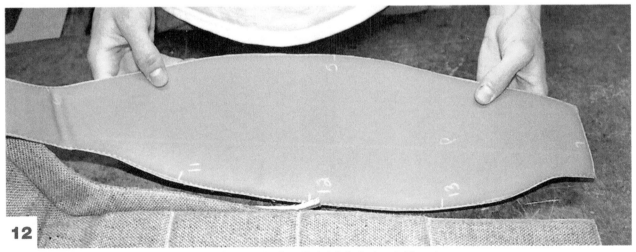

12

Remember those reference marks? On this side panel, the reference marks align with pleats in the front panel of the seat cover.

13

With both adjacent pieces positioned face to face, sew the edges of each piece of material together. To ensure proper alignment, start at the middle reference point and sew toward one end. Then go back to the middle and sew toward the opposite end.

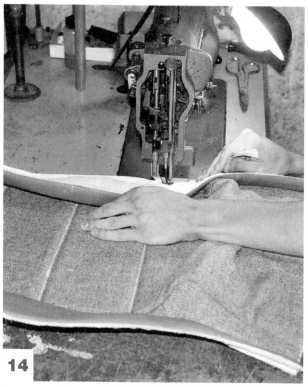

14

Sew on the opposite side panel using the same procedure. Align the reference marks, begin sewing in the middle, and work toward the ends.

15

Many upholsterers neglect tying the threads at the end of a seam. This extra step doesn't take much time, and it helps keep seams from pulling loose.

16

The seat cushion cover can now be tried on for a test fit. Verify that the cover is square with the cushion and is pulled down snug at all edges.

17

These seats originally had a piece of J-shaped hard plastic sewn onto the front edge of the seat cover. The plastic hooked onto the bottom of the molded foam seat cushion to secure the cover in place. That piece has been removed from the original cover and sewn in place on the new cover.

18

The back of the seat cushion cover is secured to the molded foam seat cushion with hog rings. To give the hog rings something to attach to, a piece of listing is glued to the underside of the seat cushion cover. A thin steel wire has been slid through this listing. The hog rings wrap around this and other wires in the cushion, securing the seat cushion cover in the process.

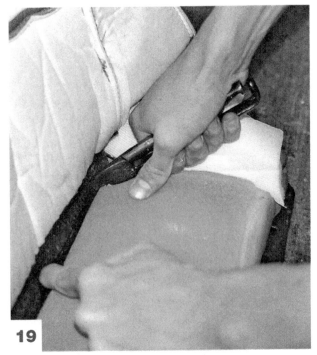

19

To help delineate the bolsters on the front and sides of the seat cushion, a piece of heavy-gauge wire stretches across the back of the front bolster and on the inside of the side bolsters and is hooked onto the bottom of the seat frame. Another wire passes through listing material (the black strip) on the seat cushion cover. This wire and the corresponding wire at the front bolster are hog ringed together.

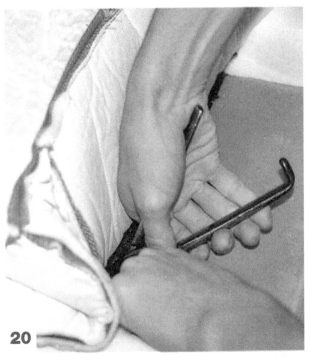

20

Use a pair of hog ring pliers and hog rings to secure the seat cushion cover to the molded foam seat cushion. Make sure that the hog ring goes around the wire in the listing.

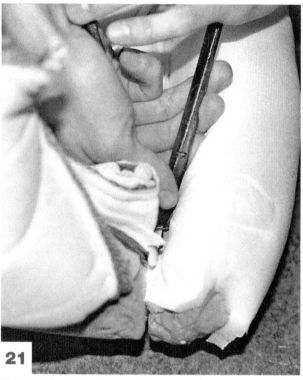

21

Similar to the front bolster, the seat cushion cover is hog-ringed to the wire that forms the side bolster. If not for these wires, the material would simply stretch across the foam, losing the shape of the bolster in the process.

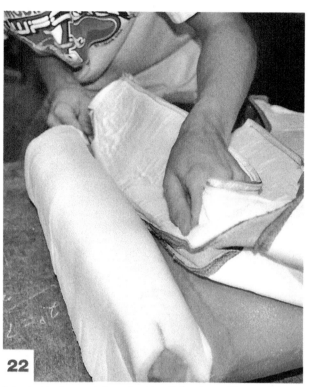

22

Before hooking the cover to the seat cushion with hog rings, pull the material flush to the side of the seat.

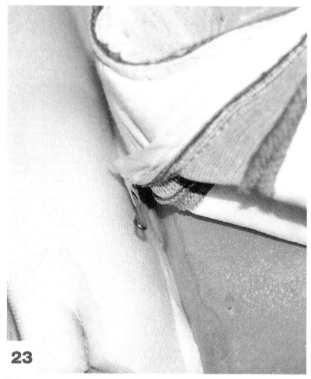

23

In the middle of the photo, you can see wire that will be hog-ringed to the wire across the seat cushion.

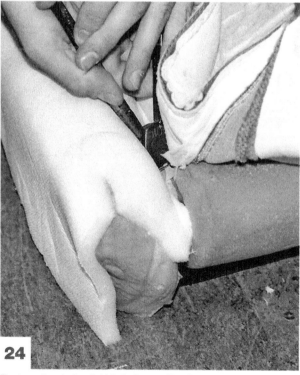

24

The deeper the wire is pulled into the foam cushion of the seat, the more pronounced the bolster will be. This makes it more difficult to attach the hog rings, but it's merely part of the job.

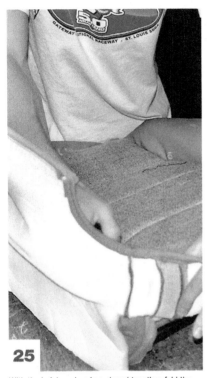

25

With the bolster wires hog-ringed together, fold the front and side flaps of the seat cushion cover over the edge of the seat.

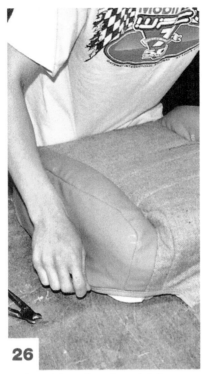

26

Check the seat cover for any low spots in the seat cushion. They will need to be filled with foam padding.

27

If the front of the seat is not full enough, cut a piece of open-cell foam to the desired size.

28

Prior to fastening the J-clips to the seat frame, stuff any extra foam between the formed seat cushion and the seat cushion cover. Flatten the foam as necessary so that it blends into the area where it is needed. It shouldn't look like a wadded-up ball of foam within the cushion.

29

Secure the seat cushion by hooking the plastic J-clips over the edges of the metal seat frame beneath the seat. It doesn't matter if you start on the sides or the front and back. Work your way around the seat cushion by attaching parallel sides before attaching the remaining perpendicular sides.

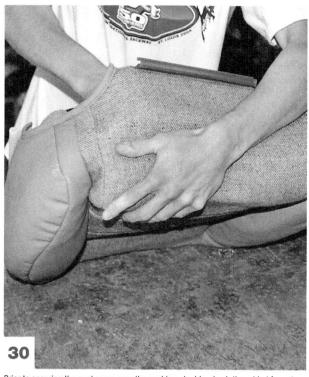

30

Prior to securing the seat cover over the cushion, double-check the added foam to make sure it has not moved out of position. It is better to go back and fix something now than to fix it later.

31

The front of the seat cushion looks much better now that extra foam has been added and is properly positioned.

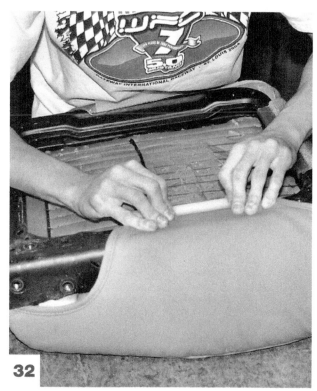

32

Hook the sides into place with J-clips. The two holes in the seat frame are for bolts that mount the hinge mechanism. They are left uncovered by upholstery material to prevent binding.

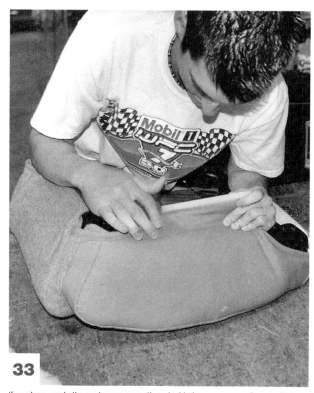

33

If you have made the seat cover correctly and added any necessary foam to fill in low spots in the molded seat cushion, the last side of the seat cushion cover should be a snug—but not tight—when pulled into position with the J-clips.

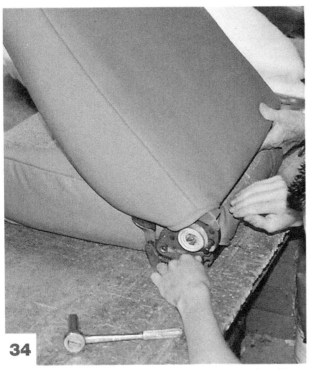

34

With the seat cushion and seat back covered, reassemble the two portions of the seat. When disassembling seats, it's a good idea to take some photos to refer to during reassembly.

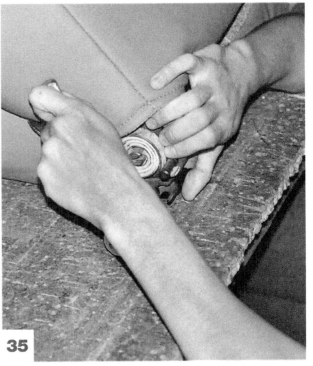

35

With these seats, reassembly consists of simply bolting the hinge mechanism to both the seat cushion and the seat back. A ratchet and a correctly sized socket make easy work of this job. Be sure to start all bolts by hand to verify that they are not cross-threaded.

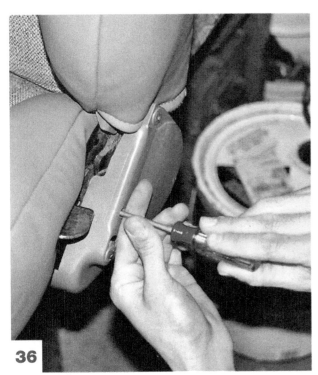

36

The hinge mechanism is usually covered by a formed piece of metal or plastic trim. The trim is held in place by a few small screws that are easily reinstalled with a screwdriver. You might need a Phillips, Torx, or other specialty screwdriver.

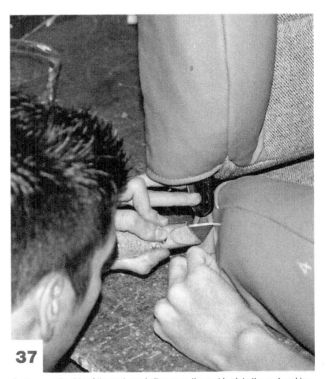

37

On the opposite side of the seat, one bolt secures the seat back to the seat cushion. To gain access to the hole into which the bolt will be inserted, use a razor knife to cut a small slit in the vinyl material that covers the seat cushion. Feel around for the hole before arbitrarily cutting a slit in the new upholstery.

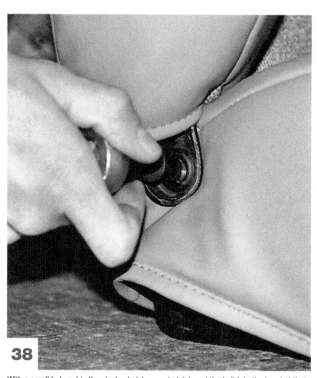

38 With a small hole cut in the vinyl upholstery material, insert the bolt into the bracket that attaches the upholstery to the seat cushion. Start the bolt by hand to make sure that no upholstery material is in the way. Tighten the bolt fully with a wrench.

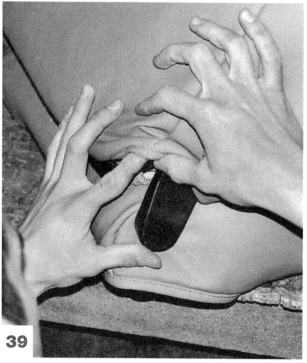

39 As on the first side, a piece of plastic or metal trim is used to cover the mounting brackets. Instead of mounting with screws, this plate is designed to snap in place over the heads of the bolts being covered.

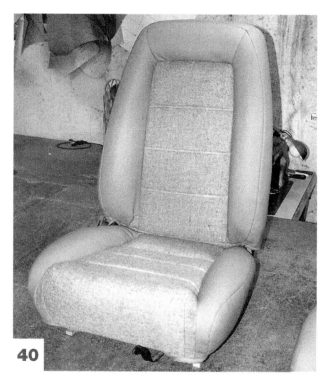

40 This is the completed seat prior to being reinstalled in the vehicle. Although we don't show the procedure for making the seat back cover, it is the same procedure used to make the seat cushion.

41 Although they are simple to make, the seat risers/mounting brackets on these seats are the first of their kind that I remember seeing. They are made of aluminum and shaped to give the desired seat angle when bolted in place in the vehicle. Holes through the very front and very back allow them to be bolted to the vehicle's floor. Similar holes in the top half allow them to be bolted to the seat frame.

Chapter 4
Door Panels

Door panels began as a simple method of covering window riser and door latch access holes on the inside of automobile doors. Upholstery covering these panels varies from non-existent to extremely elaborate. Pickup trucks manufactured through the early 1960s had non-upholstered door panels. Most simply had a steel panel that could be removed to access door and window mechanisms. The panel was usually painted the same color as the rest of the interior, or a complementary color. A step up from this bare bones approach was to upholster the panel with vinyl or tweed.

The next generation of door panels was made of molded plastic and matched the color of the car interior. As the quality of the trim on any particular model increased, door panels followed suit, including some upholstered inserts and sometimes even carpet on the lower portion of the panel. Contemporary door panels are usually made of molded composite material in a neutral color or covered with the same material as the rest of the interior.

Contemporary door panels still cover access holes, but also cover various conveniences such as armrests, door pulls, map pockets, stereo speakers, and, perhaps most importantly for car buyers, cup holders. Door panels are not complicated but can serve as a great opportunity to showcase your upholstery talents and to personalize your vehicle at the same time. Auto manufacturers learned a long time ago that many car buyers will gladly pay extra for an SS, Mustang, Super Bee, or similar emblem stitched into the upholstery of their favorite automotive dream machine.

In many newer vehicles, controls for power door locks, power windows, power mirrors, and other electronic devices are located in the door panels. On such vehicles, it is doubly important to remove and reinstall door panels properly. Not only is the door panel an upholstery item, it is also an electrical component.

REMOVAL AND REINSTALLATION

Removing door panels can be baffling if you don't keep up with how auto manufacturers attach them to doors. Many door panels are secured by screws that are easy to find, making the panels easy to remove. However, more and more contemporary vehicles use hidden clips of various styles to secure the door panels. If you cannot readily see screws securing a door panel, you might need to consult a vehicle-specific repair manual to find the hidden fasteners. You might also need a specific clip removal tool. Avoid using excessive force to remove hidden clips, because if you break any, replacements can be difficult to find.

Old Chevrolets (and presumably other cars) from the mid-1930s through the early 1960s used serrated nail clips to hold door panels in place. These clips are difficult to remove without damaging them. The originals were strips of metal with nails attached. The strips went around the entire perimeter of the door panels. Replacements are available, but they consist of short strips with a single nail in each strip. Placement of these strips on the panel is critical. They must align with small slits in the door's inner sheet metal.

MAKING CUSTOM DOOR PANELS

While contemporary vehicles commonly have door panels made of molded composite materials, you can make replacement panels for most any vehicle. You might not be able to exactly re-create the molded panels of a late-model vehicle, but with a little effort you can craft something every bit as nice. The more sculpted the panel, the more work is required, but the project is still relatively easy.

If the door panel is going to be rectangular, such as on a Model A Ford, you could take a few measurements and transfer them directly to the panel quite easily. Where angles or curves come into play, you should first make a pattern out of chipboard or poster board. You can do this by either cutting a piece of board that is too large and cutting it down to the correct size and shape or by taping pieces of board together until you get the correct size and shape. Position the scrap pieces of board around the edges of the door and hold them in place with masking tape to establish the outer limits of the door panel. Cut the corners as necessary to achieve the correct fit. Then tape pieces in the middle to fill out the pattern. When the pattern is complete, transfer it onto a piece of plywood, Masonite, or panel board material that is approximately 1/8 inch thick. Use the appropriate cutting tools and safety equipment.

The wooden door panels of this woody show how simple a door panel can (and should) be for this particular vehicle. In this photo, we can see that the panel is secured to the door with easily accessible screws. You might never need to construct a new panel like this, but might need to know how to remove or install one.

Test fit the door panel to the door. Be sure to allow for the additional thickness of any foam padding, upholstery material, and weather stripping. Determine how the panel is going to be secured to the door before going much further. If the door has threaded holes, screws of the appropriate size can be used. If square or irregular holes make finding the appropriate screw difficult, plastic clips that fit the holes and are threaded for screws are available. In other words, you might need to do some research to find the best fastener for your project. Your local auto parts store should have a small variety of fasteners; fasteners are less expensive when purchased in bulk through an upholstery supply house.

Whether you are using prefabricated door panels or making your own, they must be the correct size. They cannot extend past the edges of the door at any location, as this will obviously make the door difficult to open. Almost any material for door panels can be shrunk slightly by shaving off some of the edges with an electric or pneumatic grinder or file. If you ignore the fact that door panels are too large and attempt to force them to fit around the edges, the panels will begin to bow. If plastic clips are used to secure the door panels to doors, they'll eventually break due to the stress.

Now is the time to cut the door panel to allow for door handle movement on newer-style doors or to drill a hole for the door handle shaft on older-style doors. In the latter style, mark the radius of the door handle on the door panel prior to planning the final layout of armrests or anything else that might interfere with handle movement. Do so for riser handles as well. On older vehicles where the door handle simply slips over a round spline or square shaft, the handle can be set at most any orientation around the axis. Such handles normally hang straight down while the door is latched, but nothing says they have to be. This is good to know if you begin

running into interference issues with armrests. Extending the handle upward may provide the extra room to make the armrest actually work. Note that door latch handles usually require only 30 to 45 degrees of movement, while window riser handles require a full 360 degrees of movement.

With the panel cut to fit and a method to secure it to the door determined, the actual layout of the door panel may begin. Determine where features such as armrests, door pulls, and stereo speakers will be placed. When placing armrests, give some thought as to how the main driver will sit in the vehicle. For example, I commonly drive with my left forearm resting on the window opening in my pickup truck. In my wife's vehicle, where the seat sits lower (compared to the window opening), the window opening is a bit too high, yet the armrest is a bit too low to be comfortable for me for extended periods. These are minor annoyances, but

If you look closely where the "V" and the "8" overlap, you can see that even though they are covered with the same material, they are two distinctly different layers, showcasing a little craftsmanship in the otherwise simple door panel.

if you are redesigning the interior space anyway, you might as well get it as comfortable as can be. Remember, auto manufacturers design vehicles for the masses, making ideal comfort obtainable by only a small percentage of end users.

You must decide if the armrest is going to be covered separately from the door and then attached prior to final assembly or if the armrest will be an integral portion of the door panel. Armrests are available in a variety of shapes, sizes, and materials, or you can make your own. Separate armrests can usually be drilled and tapped to accept a couple of bolts from the back of the door panel after it is covered but prior to being installed on the door.

Door pulls are an essential part of your door panel. Unless you have a chauffeur to close the door behind you, you will need some way to pull the door closed. Model A Fords utilized a small tab in the door window garnish molding. Other vehicles used a pull strap or handle, while some used the armrest as a door pull. Any of these methods work better than rolling down the window just to close the door. Make sure the door pull is securely attached to the door and that attachment bolts are tight.

Stereo speakers can be mounted in doors but with certain precautions. Anytime electrical wiring (including speaker wires) passes through sheet metal, rubber grommets are needed to prevent rough edges in the sheet metal from chafing the wire's insulation and causing an electrical short. Allow enough slack in the wires to account for the movement of the door as it opens and closes. To avoid having wires pass from the body shell to a movable door, you can purchase aftermarket electrical contacts that make contact only while the door is closed. Since doors are prone to slamming shut, extra care must be taken when mounting speakers to make sure they stay secured to the door. In nonmoving panels, mount speakers using standard nuts and bolts. In constantly moving door panels, use locknuts or lock washers to secure the speakers and prevent damage.

Now that you have determined the location of all the extra features for your door panels, you can now decide what pattern to use in your upholstery. Do you want the panel to simply be covered or do you want to add pleats to give it some depth? Does the seat upholstery have a design that can be carried over to the door panel as well? Is the door panel going to be covered with the same material in its entirety or will you use multiple fabrics? You might want to tape a piece of drawing paper over your door panel and sketch several designs on it before deciding. Be sure to mark reference points on the door panel, the pattern, and ultimately on the fabric covering the door panel, so that everything will align when you are finished. Make enough alignment marks so that the covering can be glued in place one-half at a time.

Covering the door panel can be done with or without a sewing machine, depending on how you design the pattern. If you want to cover the door panel with tuck and roll or any type of sewn pattern, you will make a cover much like you would for a seat and then secure it to the door panel. On the other hand, you can make a sculptured door panel by gluing upholstery material to various layers of door panel material (plywood, Masonite, or whatever you are using for backing).

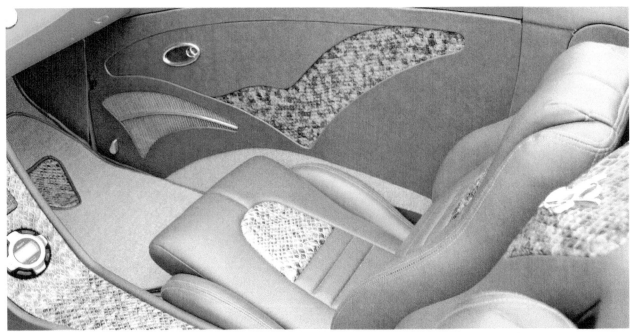

This is a busy interior. The door panels are made of multiple panels covered in a variety of materials. The bulk of the panels are covered in vinyl that is similar to if not the same as the material as used to cover the seats. The large opening in the door panel includes one insert that is covered in a similar fashion and another that is covered with exotic leather. Additional inserts are covered with carpeting and a thin speaker fabric.

Many door panels in contemporary vehicles feature multiple fabric types in flowing patterns. These can be created by cutting the door panel backing material into multiple pieces, covering each of them, and reattaching them to form the complete door panel.

For the most part, door panels are designed so that each fabric is on a different layer than the adjacent fabric. This way, the edges of material or fabric are concealed behind the layers in front of them, which are typically wrapped around the edge of the door. By covering the door panel backing board with a layer of foam and cutting away a portion of that foam, you have instantly created a sculptured door panel. Of course, you will want to do more than this, but your creativity is essentially your only restriction.

For a very simple door panel, add different thicknesses or layers of high-density foam to a door panel backing board. Then shave away portions to make it look like the outer surface of the door panel is all made from the same piece of foam.

When the panel has been cut out to the appropriate size and shaped as you wish, it needs to be covered with closed-cell foam padding prior. Cut a piece of 1/4- or 3/8-inch-thick closed-cell foam padding large enough to cover the entire door panel. Spray the back of the padding and the front of the door panel with contact cement. Let it become tacky. Position the foam padding on the door panel and begin pressing it into place. Start in the middle and work toward the edges, making sure that all wrinkles are pressed out of the foam. Cut off any excess foam padding at the edge of the door panel.

Next, cut a piece of fabric (tweed or vinyl work best) large enough to cover the door panel, plus 1 or 2 inches around the edges. Fold the fabric over on itself and spray half the back with contact cement. Spray the appropriate portion of the door panel with spray adhesive. Let it become tacky. Press the fabric into place on the door panel, making sure the fabric extends past the edges. Working outward from the middle, press any wrinkles out of the fabric. Make sure the fabric makes good contact with the foam padding over the entire surface area. Use a small roller to achieve even pressure over the entire door panel.

Apply spray adhesive on the back of the remaining half of the fabric and onto the front of the remainder of the door panel. Press the fabric into place when the spray adhesive becomes tacky. When the front of the door panel is finished, apply spray adhesive to the back of the door panel and to the back of the remaining material. Wrap the material over the edge of the panel and press it into place on the back. You will need to cut small slits into the material to prevent it from puckering when you press around corners. Just be sure the cuts don't extend onto the front.

Leave approximately 1 inch of material glued to the back of the door panel, and use a razor knife to cut and remove the excess. If you do this properly, no one will know you didn't cover a custom-molded door panel. When making a multilayered panel such as this, the key is to avoid intricate shapes, opting for

This sculptured door panel is made from one piece of backing material, some foam padding, a bit of carpet, and three pieces of vinyl. The only portion that requires the use of a sewing machine is the welting around the carpet at the bottom. The pieces of teal green, light gray, and dark gray vinyl are wrapped around foam that has been glued to the portion of the panel backing cut to that same shape

more smooth, large curves. For more on door panels, refer to the "Repairing OEM Door Panels" and the "Making Custom Door Panels" projects on pages 108 and 118.

DYEING OR REPAINTING OEM DOOR PANELS

Not all vehicles have upholstered door panels. In some vehicles, you'll need to install plastic door panels that are not covered with fabric. Additionally, in many contemporary vehicles, several pieces of the interior are made of molded vinyl. They can be painted a different color to match a new interior or repainted the same color for a fresh look. Molded vinyl is commonly found in door panels, dash panels, floor consoles, and armrests. Sometimes it is used as a protective panel on the backside of front seats. It is also found on seat belt retractor housings and on some doorsill plates. On some vehicles it is used as a complete interior covering.

You can get plastic interior panels from a restoration equipment vendor or a collision repair vendor, although they may not be available in the desired color. Not to worry—most automotive paint and supply stores carry paint designed especially for plastic or vinyl door panels. Be sure to follow the manufacturer's instructions for application and to acquire any specialty tools or materials necessary for the job.

Proper surface preparation and cleanliness is the key to any good paint job. Remove any and all dirt, grease, wax, or contaminants to make sure the paint properly adheres. Wash the parts to be painted with warm soapy water and a small scrub brush. Rinse the pieces thoroughly with clean water, and then wash and rinse again. Wipe the parts with wax and grease remover and dry them with a clean cloth. Apply primer and paint according to the manufacturer's instructions and allow the proper curing time between coats.

PROJECT 6
Repairing OEM Door Panels

 Time: 4–6 hours

 Skill Level: Medium

 Cost: Medium

 Tools & Materials: Open-cell foam padding, spray adhesive, razor knife, razor blade, pneumatic stapler, screwdriver, hammer, prongs, plastic fasteners, screws, preferred cover material

A Sew Fine Interiors customer owns an older Mustang undergoing some upgrades. It has been repainted and is ready for a new convertible top, seat covers, and door panels. The door panels are going to be covered with black vinyl, along with a medium gray tweed insert and gray carpet at the bottom. This is a very easy and common upgrade that can be done without a sewing machine.

Use the original OEM door panel as a template for cutting a piece of 1/2-inch-thick open-cell foam. Cut the foam with a razor knife.

The bluish-green panel is the bottom of the OEM door panel and will be covered with gray carpet later. The hole immediately in front of Jerry is a mounting hole for the stereo speaker. Mark portions of the foam that need to be cut out before the foam is glued to the OEM door panel.

After flipping the foam over, apply spray adhesive to the back of the foam padding. The adhesive is a little difficult to see in photographs, but it typically has a yellowish color to it that is easy to see in person. Even and complete coverage is critical for the best results.

After applying spray adhesive to the foam, apply it to the OEM door panel in the same method. Most adhesive used in upholstery work is contact cement, which must be applied to both pieces that are being glued together.

5
Turn the foam panel so the finished side is facing out and press it into place. Use your hands to smooth out any wrinkles and to ensure that both materials make good contact with each other.

6
Use a single-edge razor blade and pull the excess foam over it, cutting along the edge of the OEM panel. Always exercise caution with open razors.

7
Continue cutting the rest of the excess foam from what is glued to the door panel. While this scrap piece of foam is long and skinny, the bulk of it can be used elsewhere on this or another project.

8
On the back of the panel, cut the foam away from any speaker holes or other gaps in the paneling (such as door handle mechanisms or power window controls).

9 Cut a piece of black vinyl large enough to cover the bulk of the door panel. Remember that a piece of carpet will cover the extreme lower portion of the door panel. Place the vinyl into the proper position to cover the correct portion of the door panel.

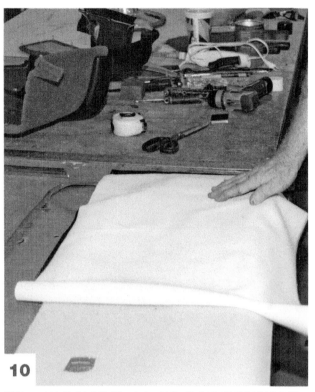

10 Fold over approximately half of the vinyl, exposing the front of half the foam and the back of half the vinyl. Spray adhesive to the back of the vinyl.

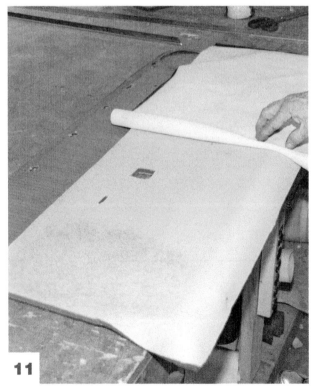

11 Apply adhesive to the face of the foam as well. After it becomes tacky, unfold the vinyl and press it back into place, smoothing it with your hands.

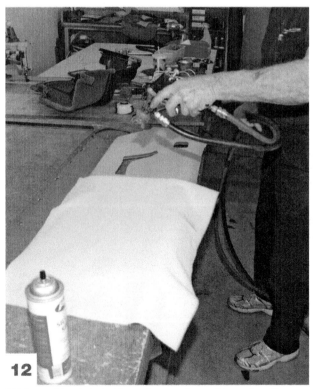

12 Fold the remaining vinyl out of the way to expose the remaining portion of the foam-covered door panel.

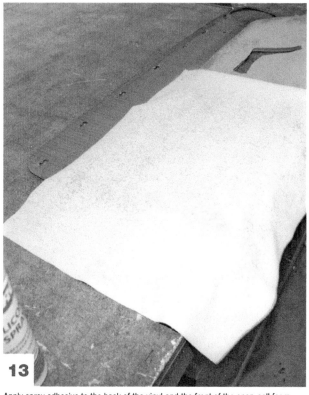

13 Apply spray adhesive to the back of the vinyl and the front of the open-cell foam.

14 After pressing out any wrinkles in the vinyl, use a staple gun to secure the lower edge of the vinyl to the door panel.

15 Staple the entire length of the lower edge of the vinyl. The staples should be about 1 inch apart. They will eventually be covered by carpet.

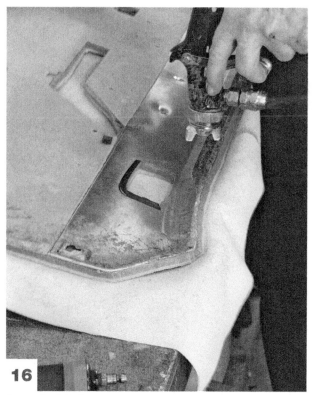

16 Because the vinyl will be wrapped up and over the top edge of the door panel, apply spray adhesive to the backs of the vinyl and the door panel.

17

Since both sides are face-up, the spray adhesive can be applied to both surfaces at the same time.

18

Pull the vinyl over the edge of the door panel and press it into place on the back of the door panel. Begin in the middle and work your way toward each edge.

19

As you work toward the front of the door panel, pressing the vinyl in place becomes more tedious. Depending on the shape of the door panel, it might be necessary to cut some slits in the material to allow it to lie flat on the back of the door panel.

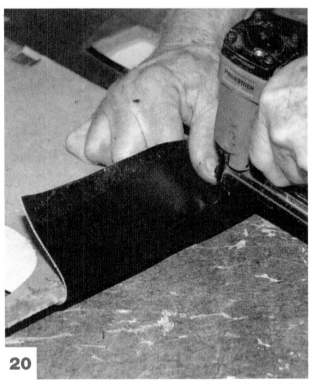

20

After working past the sheet metal backing on the top edge of the door panel, staple the vinyl to the fiberboard door panel. Be sure to use short staples that will not protrude through the face of the vinyl.

21

After gluing and stapling the vinyl to the back of the door panel, cut off any excess material.

22

After working toward the rear of the door panel, glue and staple the vinyl to the back of the door panel, just as you did in the front. You might have to trim away excess material to allow the vinyl to lie flat.

23

Trimming away excess vinyl allows the material to lie flat, thus allowing the door panel to fit properly. After stapling the vinyl to the fiberboard, trim any excess here as well.

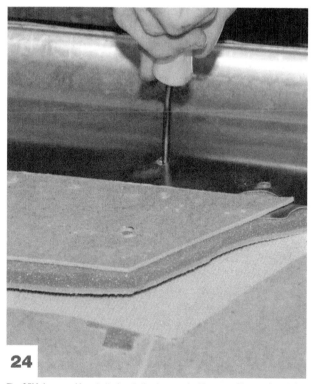

24

The OEM door panel insert attaches to the door panel with prongs. They are inserted through the door panel and then folded over on the back. Use an awl, ice pick, or pointed screwdriver to poke a small hole in the vinyl where each hole is located.

25 This is the OEM door panel insert with its attachment prongs. I don't believe this panel was re-covered, but re-covering is easy enough. Simply remove any old material, spray adhesive, and wrap the panel with new material. Fold the prongs to about 90 degrees to the angle of the insert.

26 Press the insert into place from the front. Verify that all prongs are inserted through the door panel so that no portion of the insert is loose.

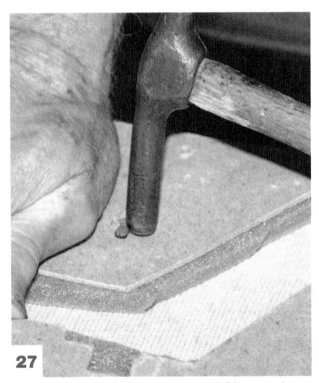

27 Flip the door panel over so that the prongs are accessible. Fold them over by hand. Then tap them with a hammer to secure them tight against the back of the door panel.

28 The door panel is almost finished, needing just the carpet installed along the lower edge to be complete. A piece of carpet long enough and tall enough has already been cut.

29

Begin the carpet installation by spraying adhesive onto the back of the carpet.

30

Apply adhesive to the front of the door panel where the carpet will be. With the stereo speaker opening removing a good portion of the contact area, apply the adhesive a little heavier around the border of the speaker hole. With experience comes a steady hand and good aim, allowing application of adhesive with no need to mask the adjacent vinyl.

31

Spray the rest of the exposed door panel with adhesive and position the carpet to press into place.

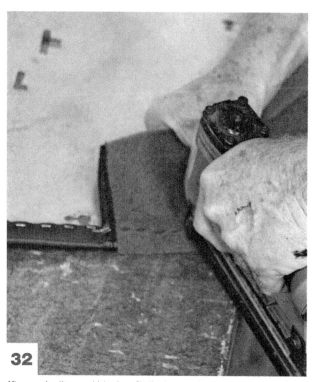

32

After pressing the carpet into place, flip the door panel over and secure it with a row of staples about 1/2 inch apart.

33

The carpet is thicker and more flexible than the vinyl, so it does not have to be slit to maneuver around the corner of the door panel. After securing the carpet with staples around the perimeter of the panel, cut away excess carpet with a single-edged razor blade.

34

Wrap the speaker cover in carpet and secure it to the door panel with screws. Unlike vinyl or leather, automotive carpet is porous. You can use it to cover stereo speakers without punching any holes in it.

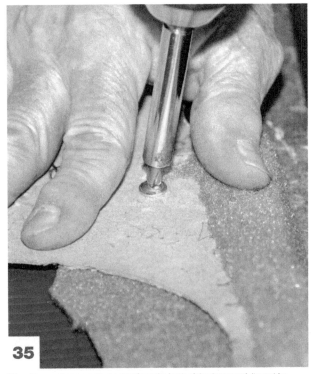

35

Since the speaker cover is secured from the back of the door panel, it must be installed prior to installing the door panel on the door. Verify that all mounting screws are in place and are tight.

36

This car was obviously red before being repainted blue. Before installing the door panel, make note of any wiring or mechanisms that need to be fed through the door panel.

37 Many door panels and other interior panels are secured with plastic fasteners similar to this one. The shaft extends through the larger flat portion equal to the thickness of the door panel.

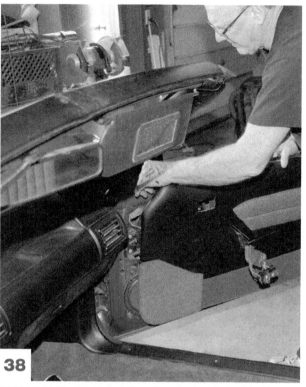

38 Hold the door in its approximate position with one hand and feed switch wiring through the door panel with the other hand.

39 Push and secure the door panel into position by aligning the plastic fasteners into their respective holes in the door's inner sheet metal.

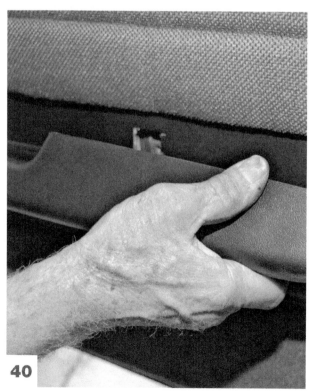

40 Install the armrest using screws located underneath it and out of view.

PROJECT 7
Making Custom Door Panels

   Time: 4–6 hours

Skill Level: Medium

Cost: Medium

 Tools & Materials: Open-cell foam padding, spray adhesive, razor blade or utility knife, upholsterer's knife, straightedge, sewing machine and thread, plastic fasteners, pneumatic stapler, small brush, preferred cover material

Sew Fine Interiors enjoys a steady group of customers who are constantly upgrading their rides, one bit at a time. One customer is ready for new door panels. The panels are made by first cutting a panel board to the correct size and shaping it to fit the door. Next, a section is cut from the middle to make ready for new material to be reinstalled into the door panel. The outer portion of the door panel is covered with multiple layers of foam and various treatments. Follow along as Jerry makes some sculptured door panels that require minimal sewing.

1 The overall door panel backing has already been cut out. The pattern has been drawn onto it, and the main insert has been cut out. Additionally, a notch for the door hinge has been cut and holes for "Christmas tree" fasteners have been punched out. You will need to do these steps for each door that you cover.

2 Place the door panel onto a roll of 1/2-inch foam. The door panel is positioned to minimize wasted foam.

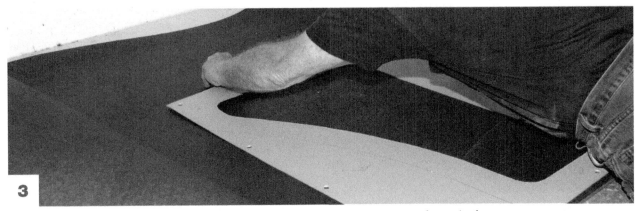

3 Cut the foam with a razor blade. Some trimmers use a utility knife, which is easier to hold onto. It is simply a matter of personal preference.

4

Apply spray adhesive to the back of the foam. Although adhesive is available in spray cans, it is cheaper when purchased in bulk and applied with a spray gun.

5

Most spray adhesive has a distinct yellow-green tint that helps trimmers verify complete coverage during application. An uncovered area or an area that is not allowed to become tacky eventually mars finished upholstery in the form of a bubble. You won't be able to get rid of it without completely redoing your work.

6

Spray adhesive is a type of contact cement, so also coat the door panel. If an airborne flake or other piece of dust or garbage lands in the adhesive, now is the time remove it. Don't cover over it.

7

Add a little more adhesive to any areas that were missed or sprayed too thin. The adhesive must become tacky to work properly, and the entire surface must be covered.

8

Turn the door panel over so that it can be positioned onto the foam. Excessive foam is indeed wasteful, but you'll need extra foam so that you don't have to be overly precise when you position the door panel.

9

After positioning the door panel on the foam, apply steady and even pressure all the way around to ensure that good and permanent contact is made between the foam and the door panel.

10

Use a razor blade or utility knife from the underside of the panel to cut away the excess foam. Some trimmers prefer to cut from the top and to simply trace around the door panel.

11

After cutting away the excess foam from around the edges of the door panel, cut away the foam in the middle of the door panel. The middle will be filled with an insert of a different color.

12 Eventually, each of the small holes will need a plastic fastener. The fasteners need to be flush with the interior of the door panel and to protrude into holes in the door's sheet metal. Refer to "Repairing OEM Door Panels" on page 117 for a photo of a plastic fastener.

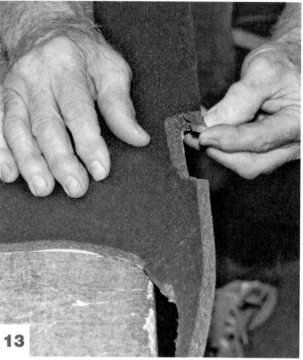

13 After cutting away the excess foam, make a second pass around the door panel with a razor blade to bevel the edge of the foam. This is a relatively minor step, but it helps to eliminate fit problems when the door panel is installed and the door has weather stripping around it. This is also necessary at recesses for door hinges.

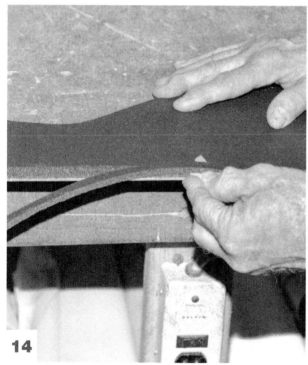

14 Beveling the edge of the foam gives the material covering the foam a softer edge that is less likely to bind and buckle (making your upholstery work look bad in the process).

15 To create more relief in the door panel and render it truly three-dimensional, remove a strip of foam from around the padded insert. This allows the finished door panel and the insert to be at the same level, with a lower strip separating the two. Use a straightedge to make the guidelines consistent.

16 A drafter's circle template makes rounding corners of guidelines easy. After marking a guideline all the way around the insert area, slice the foam along the line and then remove it.

17 Removing the narrow strip of foam creates a separation, and therefore some character, between the insert and the rest of the door panel.

18 It is not uncommon to add carpet to the lower portion of a door panel. In this case, the carpet is added only from about the front of the seat forward. Many shops have a vast collection of composite templates for repeating common shapes.

19 After marking a line parallel and concentric with the lower edge of the door panel's insert, cut the foam away from the area that will be covered with carpet. Carpeting will be installed a little later in the process.

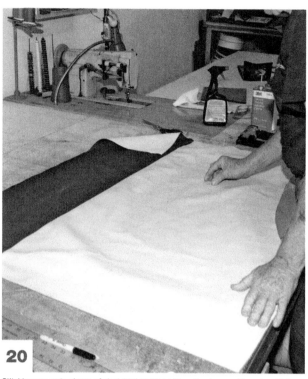

20

Stitching separate pieces of vinyl (teal and ivory) together is easy. Use a topstitch. The seam is attached to a precise line marked on the door panel. The teal material will be above the line, while the ivory material will cover the bulk of the rest of the door panel below the line.

21

Lay out your material and position it over the door panel. Fold over a little of both vinyl portions. If coating the entire underside is difficult, use spray adhesive along just the narrow strip of the seam. This will allow the seam to be positioned properly, without any other vinyl sticking to the foam.

22

Spray adhesive along the guideline on the front face of the foam. Spraying adhesive on either vinyl or foam away from the seam will inhibit the precise placement of the seam.

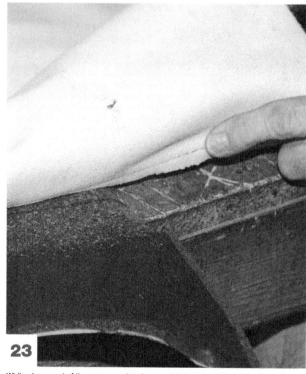

23

While placement of the seam or color change might seem arbitrary, it is chosen for a specific reason. It might correspond to a paint line break on adjacent sheet metal or to something else. If it aligns with something else, make sure it lines up correctly.

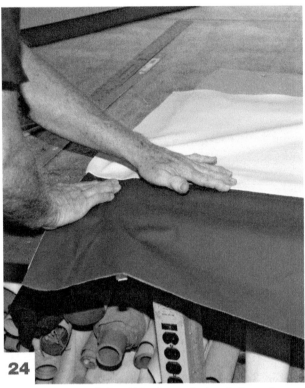

24

After aligning the seam with the guideline drawn on the foam, firmly press the material down without moving it off the line, making sure the material makes permanent contact with the foam beneath it.

25

With the seam firmly in place, spray adhesive on the upper portion of the front face of the foam.

26

Then spray adhesive on the back of the vinyl.

27

Press the vinyl into place with an open hand. While this portion of the work is not difficult, do not rush through it. Take your time and do it right.

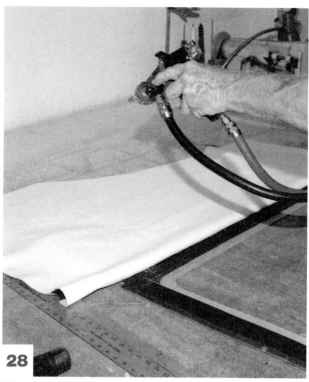

28 With the vinyl glued down, spray adhesive onto the back of the other strip of vinyl. The pattern of the door panel results in about a 3-square-foot scrap piece of material.

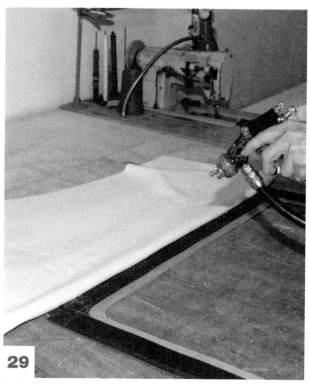

29 Apply adhesive liberally around the perimeter of the back of the vinyl, as it has only a narrow strip of door panel to hang onto. Don't apply adhesive to the middle of the vinyl, as it has nothing behind it to stick to.

30 Apply a healthy coat of adhesive to the door panel too. Besides seats and floor coverings, the door panels probably receive the most wear, making them vulnerable to visible wear-and-tear for less-than-perfect craftsmanship.

31 Jerry will work his way down the short edge and then down the longer edge with the ivory vinyl. It is important to keep a bit of tension on the material while running down these separate legs to prevent wrinkles around edge of the material.

32

Remember that the middle is going to be cut out, but you cannot have any wrinkles around the edge. Take your time and work your way out from the center.

33

Jerry pulls the material outward with his right hand as he presses the material in place with his left hand. As he works right to left in the photo, he continues to pull the material slightly to prevent wrinkles in the material.

34

Very small wrinkles can be pressed out by hand. However, anything larger will require pulling up the material, reshooting both surfaces with adhesive, and then pressing the material down again.

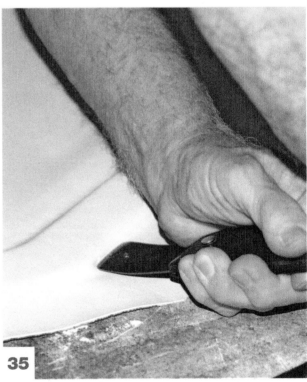

35

To add definition to the multilayer door panel, Jerry uses an upholsterer's knife to press the material completely against the layer of foam. If you do not have an upholsterer's knife, use a new putty knife with the corners ground off.

36

Crisp and consistent sure beats dull and undulating when it comes to sculptured upholstery panels. This may be a time-consuming process, but doing this step correctly and completely will make your work stand out from the also-rans.

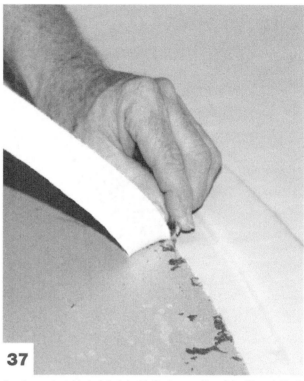

37

Jerry leaves about 1 inch of vinyl glued to the door panel board. Anything outside of that can be cut and pulled away. Eventually, carpet with a bound edge will cover the strip of vinyl, as it abuts the raised foam.

38

After all this time, the spray adhesive on the back of the vinyl and the door panel board have dried and are no longer tacky, making a new coat a necessity on both. The very middle of the vinyl doesn't need spray adhesive, since it will eventually be cut away.

39

Using a razor blade, slice the vinyl so that it can be folded over square with each side of the opening. A square opening requires only an X, while an opening with more sides requires more cuts.

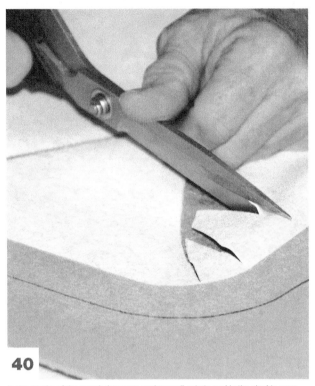

40

In the depths of the rounded corners, make small cuts to enable the vinyl to more closely fit around the curve. Do not cut vinyl any closer to the edge of the door panel board than the thickness of the board itself. If you cut closer, there will be slivers of uncovered door panel board.

41

Here we can see that vinyl will lie down nicely around curves if slices are cut out of it. Be sure to press the vinyl down firmly, so it adheres to the door panel board completely. The loose ends will be trimmed off later.

42

Pull the vinyl material taut with one hand and presses it down firmly onto the door panel board with the other hand.

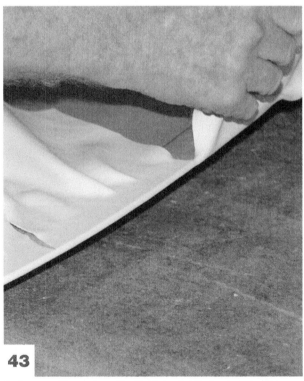

43

Continue around the opening, pulling the vinyl material taut and pressing it into place, all the way back around to the starting point.

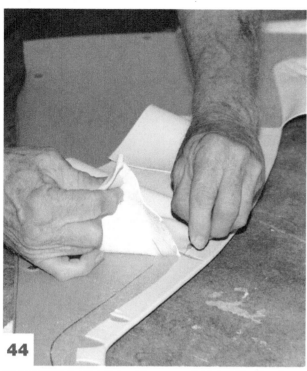

44 Use a razor blade or utility knife to cut the excess material about 1 inch from the opening. Then pull the excess material away.

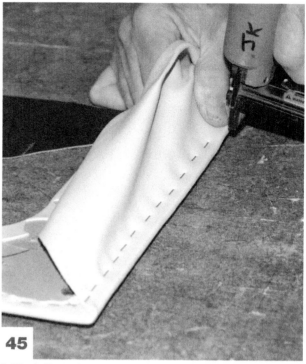

45 Pull the vinyl taut and use a pneumatic stapler to secure it to the back of the door panel along the outside edge. Leave a 1/2-inch gap between each staple. Use a razor blade or utility knife to cut the excess material just past the staples. Pull the excess material off the panel board.

46 Wrap the vinyl over the front of the door panel at the A-pillar and the top of the door panel at the window opening. Use a pneumatic stapler to install staples about a 1/2 inch apart. Do not use staples that are too long, lest they go all the way through the panel.

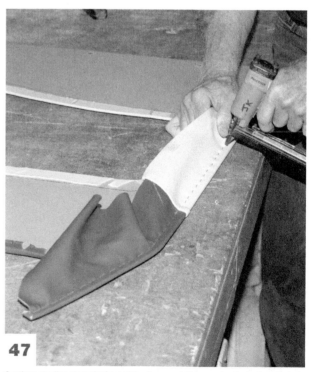

47 Continue stapling along the front of the door panel. Using many staples is not a bad thing. It helps ensure that the door panel will not need to be repaired. With the vinyl secured properly and completely to the door panel, use a single-edged razor blade or utility knife to cut away the excess material.

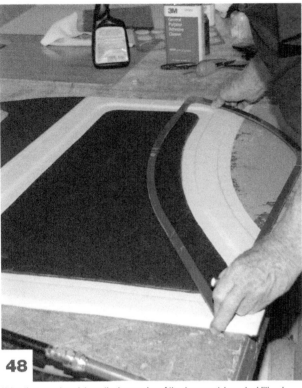

48

Using the same template as the lower edge of the door panel, lay out additional parallel and concentric lines in the closed-cell foam.

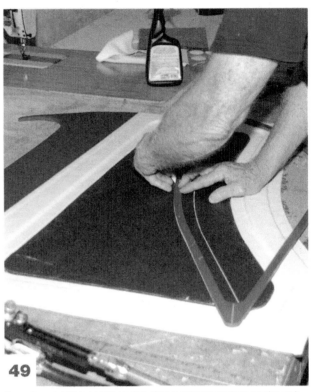

49

Use a piece of chalk to trace the outline of the template three times, spacing each outline approximately 1 1/2 inch apart.

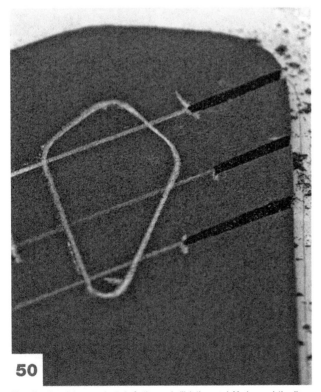

50

Use other templates or cutouts to further embellish the panel. Mark preexisting lines or patterns about 1 inch from any new additions, and cut about 1/4 inch into the foam.

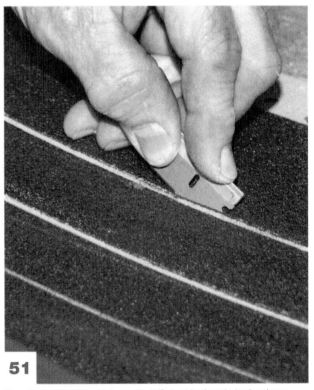

51

Use a single-edged razor blade or utility knife to make the cuts, tracing along a chalk line.

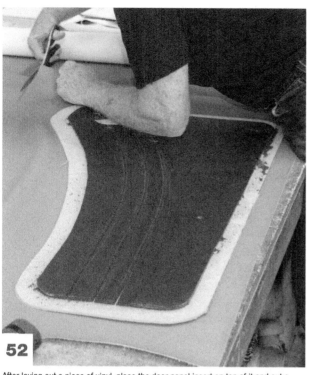

52

After laying out a piece of vinyl, place the door panel insert on top of it and cut a large enough piece of vinyl to cover the insert.

53

Position the vinyl so that it completely covers the foam. Fold the vinyl and spray adhesive to the front of the foam and the back of the vinyl.

54

Press the vinyl onto the face adjacent to the first groove or pattern. Use an upholsterer's knife to press the material into any pattern gaps. Press the material down into the pattern and repeat for subsequent patterns. Once you are finished, spray both the remaining foam and vinyl and press them into place.

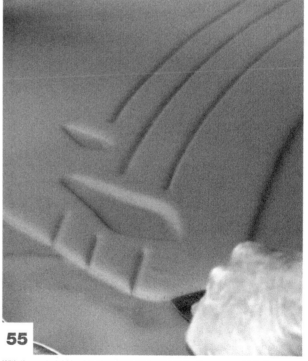

55

With the material glued in place over the foam and the foam pressed into the custom pattern, use an upholsterer's knife to press the vinyl against the outer edge of the foam. The material that covers the flange of the insert also needs to be pressed flat, as the outer ring of the door panel fits down over it. Flip the door panel insert over and trim off any excess vinyl material with a single-edged razor blade or utility knife.

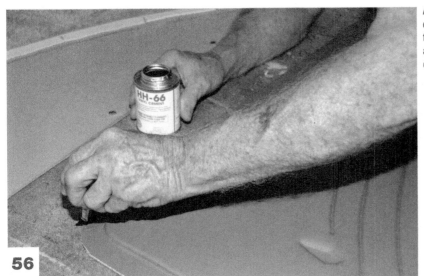

Apply contact adhesive to the front of the flange portion of the vinyl-covered insert. Since this is the front of the finished panel, use a small brush (hidden here) to carefully apply the contact adhesive to avoid coating finished exterior material with spray adhesive.

56

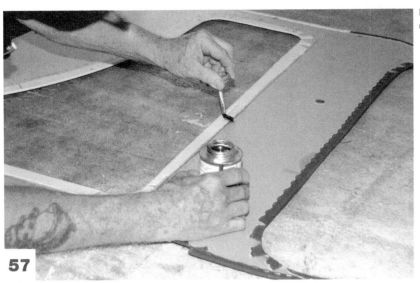

Brush contact adhesive onto the back of the outer portions of the door panel.

57

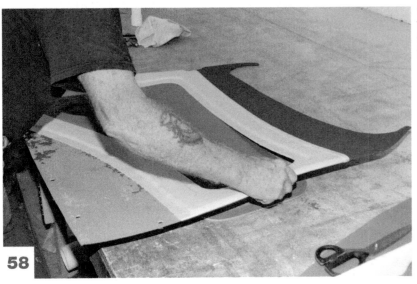

Once the adhesive is tacky, place the outer door panel on top of the panel insert. Align both panels precisely. Press down on the outer door panel to ensure that it makes good contact with the insert below.

58

To prevent obstructions from telegraphing through to the outer layer (yet to be applied), remove any residual glue or material that remains on the flange portion of the door panel insert prior to installing the carpet.

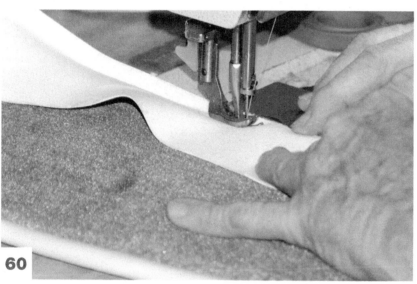

Cut a piece of carpet to fit the remaining uncovered portion of the door panel, wrap the top edge abutting the insert with a piece of vinyl, and sew it in place. This step prevents the carpeting from unraveling. Sew a wider piece of vinyl to the edges of the panel for the edge of the door.

Apply spray adhesive along the flange of the door panel insert. Carefully aim the spray gun at point-blank range to avoid over-spraying the uncovered face of the door panel.

Apply spray adhesive to the remaining portion of the uncovered door panel. Spray the back of the carpet as well.

62

Position the carpeting along the flange of the door panel insert and press it into place so that the adhesive makes good contact.

63

Prepare to secure the vinyl by rolling it over to the back of the door panel.

64

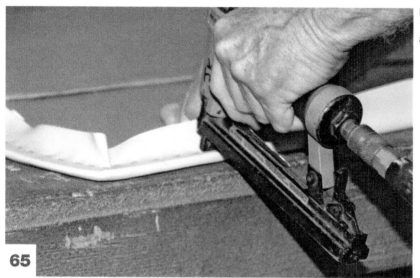

65

Pull the vinyl taut and secure it with staples spaced about 1/2 inch apart. Double-check the length of the staples to avoid shooting through the front of the panel.

66

Use a single edged-razor blade or utility knife to trim the excess vinyl material. Note that the vinyl is stapled and removed below the holes in the door panel so that it does not interfere with any fasteners used to secure the panel.

67

Insert plastic fasteners into the mounting holes in the back of the door and press the panel into place. Verify that all the fasteners are pressed into the door all the way or that the screws (if used) are actually threaded into the metal of the door.

Chapter 5
Floor Coverings

Vehicle floor coverings have certainly evolved over the years. Painted sheet metal was a big improvement over the floors of wooden buckboards and covered wagons. Because painted sheet metal becomes slippery when wet, rubber floor mats were the next improvement. While these were suitable in commercial vehicles, they were not stylish enough for passenger cars. We had wall-to-wall carpeting in our homes, so there was no reason not to have carpeting in our vehicles. Today almost all passenger cars come from the factory with carpeted floors. Most people purchase extra carpet or rubber floor mats to protect the carpeting.

PADDING

Installing carpeting without padding beneath it is only asking to shorten the lifetime of the carpet. Not only does carpet padding provide some insulating and noise-abatement properties, it allows the carpet to give somewhat, helping preserve it.

Three common types of automotive carpet padding are jute felt, polyfoam, and rebond. Jute felt is generally regarded as the best, due largely to its insulating qualities, but it is the most expensive of the three. With other superior insulating and sound-deadening products available, there is no reason to spend the extra money for jute felt padding.

Providing a good combination of material and price is polyfoam. Polyfoam is easy to use in compound curved areas of many floor pans. It doesn't crease, and it provides better insulating qualities than rebond. Made from recycled material, rebond is environmentally sound and cheaper than the other types of padding.

Regardless of which type of padding you use, it is basically installed the same way. Begin by removing seats,

In this partially completed hot rod coupe, the insulation and carpet padding are already installed. Rather than simply running the wiring on top of the padding and then covering it with carpet, cut a trough into the padding so the wiring can be pushed down into it. When the carpet or floor mats are installed, they'll be wrinkle-free.

scuff plates, shifter boots, and anything else holding down the original carpeting. Even if it is glued in place, the carpeting can usually be peeled up with ease. If it is difficult to remove in spots, check to see if it is being held by something that needs to be removed, such as a seat belt. If the carpet appears stuck, slide a wide putty knife underneath it to release any residual glue.

Prior to discarding the old carpet, look at its back to see if it shows any seaming; this will give you an idea on how to piece the new carpeting together. If the existing carpeting still fits well (and is not stretched or torn), you might be able to use it as a pattern for both the carpet padding and the carpeting itself.

Cut a piece of carpet padding the desired size, push it into the floor pan, and center it front to back and side to side. The smaller and flatter the floor pan, the easier this becomes. Larger floor pans with more contours are more difficult. Wherever a floor shifter, brake or gas pedal, or anything else protrudes through the floor, cut slits in the padding so it can be slipped over these appendages. If a boot is used, such as for a floor shifter, you don't have to be as precise in your cutting. With carpet padding and/or carpet, cut some material away so that it does not restrict movement of the shifter, clutch, brake, gas pedal, or any other device.

Cut the padding to the correct size and position it appropriately. Fold approximately half of it over on itself and apply spray adhesive to both the floor and the back of the padding. When the spray adhesive becomes tacky, push the padding into place. Now fold the other half of the padding over and repeat. Trim off any excess padding that remains.

In most vehicles, covering the transmission hump and driveshaft tunnel is the biggest obstacle when installing floor covering, because of their conical shape. Limiting your work to front-wheel drive vehicles eliminates part of the problem, but it also minimizes your opportunity to gain experience with different types of vehicles—and we don't want that. It may be necessary to cut multiple pieces of padding to properly fit these two obstacles and then separately cover each side of the floor pan.

If any wiring runs across the floor where padding has been installed, you must deal with it now, or it will look like a snake is trapped under the carpeting. Taking care to not cut through any wiring, cut along both sides of the wiring to form a trough in the carpet padding. Position the wires in the trough below the surface of the padding, providing a smooth surface for the carpet to lie on. For more on carpet padding, refer to the "Installing Carpet Padding" project on page 140.

CARPETING

Most automotive carpeting is either of the loop or cut pile variety. Blended loop carpeting is a combination of materials, usually rayon and nylon. This type of carpeting was used extensively in most domestic vehicles from the 1950s through the early 1970s. Cut pile carpeting, usually nylon or more expensive Wilton wool, is commonly found in vehicles manufactured from the early 1970s to the present.

Measuring

The carpeting might be torn, you might be working on a custom vehicle that doesn't have old carpeting, or you might just want to know how to measure correctly, so I'll tell you how it should be done. Measure the floor front to back and side to side and allow about an extra 20 percent each way. Remember that carpeting typically rises up the inside the firewall far enough that no bare firewall is seen by anyone in the front seat. Measure accurately to purchase the correct amount of padding and carpeting.

Cutting

For most vehicles, three pieces of carpeting need to be cut. The first piece covers the transmission hump, while the other two cover the floor on either side of it. Depending on the length and depth of the driveshaft tunnel (if present), one piece of carpeting might be able to cover both sides of the floor beside it. It may be necessary to add fourth and fifth pieces to cover each side in the rear seat area. If you do add these two last pieces in the back, for aesthetic reasons, position them so that any seam or overlap is beneath the front seat.

Rather than cutting carpet right from the start, begin by making a pattern out of Kraft or pattern paper. Roll out a piece of paper that is longer and wider than the pattern needs to be. You may need to tape multiple pieces together to create a large enough pattern. Draw a centerline on the paper to represent the centerline of the transmission hump. Measure front-to-back from under the dash to the back end of the hump. Transfer this measurement to the pattern.

Where this hump meets the flat floor, some vehicles have a series of straight lines while others have a curved line. If your vehicle has a series of straight lines, measure back from a reference point along the centerline of the hump to where the hump meets the floor at each angle point. If the meeting of the hump and the floor forms a curved line, make more measurements front to back (again from a reference point) and then measure over. Then it is a matter of connecting the dots on your pattern until it looks similar to the transmission hump. From the first line representing where the transmission hump meets the flat floor, add a second line outward approximately 3 inches. Cut along this outer line to form your pattern.

Check the pattern by laying it out over the transmission hump to make sure it covers everything it is supposed to. If you have a floor shifter to contend with, locate it on the pattern as well. It is easier and less expensive to repair the pattern than the carpet if the hole for the shifter is in the wrong place.

Measure each side of the floor from the door over to the transmission hump. Measure front to back under the dash to the underside of the back seat. Add about 3 inches in each direction to allow for imperfections, which can be trimmed off later. If you're using separate pieces in the rear, measure from the middle of the area beneath the front seat to under the back seat. Be sure to indicate on the patterns which way is front and which side is which.

Cut out all the patterns and lay them on the carpeting. Situate them so that the arrows on all the pieces point to the front of the vehicle. Carpeting has a directional nap, similar to grain in wood. You always want the nap to run in the same direction. Use a piece of chalk to mark the outline of the pattern on the carpeting. Cut the carpeting with a sharp pair of shears.

Binding

Sometimes it is necessary to bind the edge of the carpeting, such as anytime more than one piece of carpeting is being used or when a rough edge is not covered by a doorsill plate or shifter boot. First, measure the length of binding needed. Cut a piece of vinyl or leather approximately 2 inches wide to the necessary length. Place the binding material face down on the upper side of the carpet and align the edges. From this common edge, measure inward 1/2 inch and stitch the length of the binding. Apply glue to the back of the carpet from the edge to approximately 1 1/2 inches from the edge. Fold the binding material over the edge so that the carpeting is covered. Press the binding in place on the back of the carpeting until the adhesive is dry. Once the glue is dry, stitch along the finished edge of the carpeting through the binding on the back to make the binding permanent.

INSTALLING

Begin by positioning the center piece of carpet over the transmission hump. Center it side to side and make sure the carpet rises high enough on the inside of the firewall and far enough under the back seat to hold it into position. If you made your pattern correctly, about 3 inches of carpeting should extend onto the flat portion of the floor on each side.

On vehicles with a floor shifter, cut a small hole in the carpet so it can slide down over the shifter. If the shifter has a removable boot, cut the carpet a little more to ease installation over the shifter knob, as the raw edges of the carpet can be covered by the boot. If there is no removable shifter boot, make short radial cuts in the carpet to allow it to pass over the shifter. Sew a piece of binding around the hole through which the shifter protrudes. If you do not have a floor shifter, covering the transmission hump is practically done.

Where the transmission hump turns upward to the firewall to cover the transmission's bell housing, additional work is required to obtain a good fit. Press the carpet firmly into the crease formed by the vertical portion of the firewall and the horizontal portion of the floor. At this crease, fold the upper portion of the carpet (the part that will cover the

firewall) backward toward the rear of the vehicle. Cut along this crease from the bottom of the driver side to the bottom of the passenger side. With the 3 inch overlap on either side of the transmission hump, only one piece of carpet remains— the piece with the slit. Sew a piece of carpet binding to the back edge of this cut. (If the very front of the carpet is at the top and the back is at the bottom, the binding should be placed on the bottom of the top portion of carpeting.) When the carpeting is installed, the finished edge will cover the raw edge due to the change in direction of the carpeting from horizontal to vertical.

Glue the carpet in place and fold one side of the carpet onto itself. Spray adhesive onto the back of the carpet and onto the exposed floor. Press the carpet into place after the adhesive becomes tacky. Repeat the process for the opposite side.

Move on to the passenger-side carpeting. Lay the carpeting in place, making sure its edge lines up with the outer edge of the floor. Secure the edge by placing the doorsill plate on it and then fastening it with screws. Trim the edge to fit properly before making any cuts on the inboard side. With the carpet positioned properly, cut it in the crease where the front part of the floor pan meets the rounded portion in front of the transmission hump, and along the crease between the transmission hump and the floor. Sew a binding edge along the front and inboard edge of the passenger-side carpeting. Cut the carpet as necessary to clear the seat mounting/sliding mechanisms and seat belt mounting holes. Secure the carpet with the doorsill plate at the doorway and by applying spray adhesive to the inboard half.

The driver-side carpet is installed the same way. However, foot pedals may necessitate some additional work. Brake and clutch pedals that swing from under the dash pose no problem, but older vehicles have pedals that protrude through the floor and firewall. Some vehicles have pedal arms that are easily removed from underneath the floor. Some have pedal pads that can be removed. Either way, cut a small slit in the carpet for each pedal. Depending on the size of the slit, you might choose to sew binding around the hole. For the throttle pedal, cut a slot for the actuator cable or, if you can remove the cable, cut a hole and install a grommet. Pass the cable through the grommet and reattach the cable to the throttle pedal. You can secure the pedal to the floor through the carpet. If you have a floor-mounted dimmer switch, cut around the switch and sew a binding edge to it.

Another consideration is the choice between heel pads and floor mats. Place a heel pad where it will provide the most protection for the carpet. Trace around it with chalk. Remove the carpet and sew the heel pad into place. Secure the carpet with spray adhesive and the doorsill plate. Some trimmers prefer floor mats to heel pads. Floor mats are easier to replace and easy to remove and clean. They can be made from scrap pieces of carpet. Cut floor mats to the desired shape and size and finish them by sewing on a binding edge.

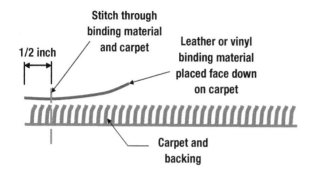

Stitch through
binding material
and carpet

Leather or vinyl
binding material
placed face down
on carpet

1/2 inch

Carpet and
backing

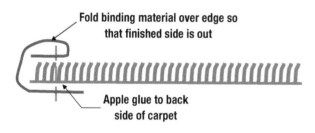

Fold binding material over edge so
that finished side is out

Apple glue to back
side of carpet

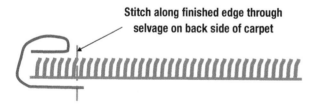

Stitch along finished edge through
selvage on back side of carpet

NOTE: Drawing is not to scale and is merely
a representation. Binding should be wrapped
smoothly around the edge of the carpeting.

This sketch shows how binding is sewn onto carpet edges left uncovered by sill
plates. Place the binding material face down on the carpet with their common edges
aligned. Stitch through both the binding material and the carpet approximately 1/2
inch from the common edge. Apply glue to the back of the carpeting and then roll
the binding material over the edge of the carpet. Add one more stitch through the
carpet and binding material on the back.

Installing Molded Carpet

For a growing list of automobiles, vehicle-specific molded carpet is available, making the installation of new carpet an easy proposition for the do-it-yourselfer.

Take the new carpeting out of the packaging and lay it as flat as possible for 12 to 24 hours at normal room temperature to return it to its original shape. Remove the car's seats, seat belts, doorsill plates, and anything else that mounts to the floor if at all possible. Remove the old carpeting but don't throw it away. Also remove the old padding. Now is a good time to vacuum the floor, gather up all the loose change, and remove all the gum wrappers, potato chip crumbs, and anything else that does not belong under the carpet.

Determine the front end from the rear end of the new carpet. A heel pad will be located directly beneath the accelerator pedal, helping you determine how the new carpeting should be oriented in the vehicle. If the new carpeting does not have a heel pad, lay the old carpeting atop the new, turning it as necessary to achieve the best fit. (On most vehicles, this should be fairly obvious.) With the old carpeting properly situated atop the new, mark any holes that need to be cut with a piece of chalk. There are typically holes for seat mounts, seat belt mounts, and possibly a floor shifter. Other holes might also need to be marked and cut.

Reinstall all the bolts that thread into the floor pan before installing the carpet into the vehicle. This step helps align the carpet, as each bolt has a corresponding chalk mark on the new carpeting. Fold or roll the new carpet as necessary to fit it through the car door, then unroll or unfold it so it lies flat. Center the carpeting over the transmission hump and transmission tunnel and then work toward the sides. With the middle of the carpet properly located, the chalk marks should align reasonably close with the heads of the bolts threaded into the floor. If they are not aligned, you might need to start over prior to making any cuts. If the chalk marks and bolt heads do line up, use a razor knife to make a slice in the carpet across the top of the bolt head. Cut just enough of the carpet for the shaft of the bolt to fit through. Push the carpet down around the bolt. Unthread the bolt enough for the carpet to fit beneath the bolt head.

After all the bolt holes are cut out, remove the bolts from approximately half of the carpet and fold that section over. Apply spray adhesive to both the floor and the back of the carpet and press the carpet back into place. Repeat this process for the rest of the carpet, trimming as necessary to fit under doorsill plates, kick panels, and other trim. Reinstall the back seat and the front seats, bolting them securely in place. Finish the job by reinstalling sill plates, seat belts, and any other trim pieces that were removed.

PROJECT 8
Installing Carpet Padding

 Time: 2–4 hours

 Skill Level: Basic

 Cost: Low

 Tools & Materials: Preferred carpet padding, sound-dampening material (optional), thermal insulation (optional), utility knife, spray adhesive, glue, chalk, shears, rubber mallet, fitting needles,

Instead of automotive carpet backing, Sew Fine Interiors uses carpet padding intended for home use. Jute felt backing has been used forever in the automotive industry, but it is largely scraps of recycled material loosely bound together and not as strong as traditional residential carpet. As it begins to fall apart, voids form beneath it. As traffic on the carpet increases over those voids, the carpet begins to show signs of fatigue. By using higher-quality residential carpet padding, premature fatigue is avoided.

Carpet padding also lets the installer fill the low spots common in stock floor pans. The padding provides a smoother substrate for the carpeting and eliminates the need for formed carpet pads that are available only for limited vehicles and in limited colors. Follow along as Brian Flynn installs carpet padding.

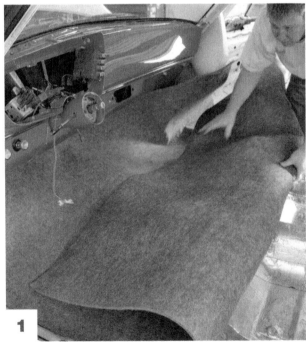

1 Install sound-dampening or thermal insulation material prior to the carpet padding. Cut a large piece of carpet padding, roll it up, put it in the vehicle, and unroll it inside. The carpet should be slightly longer and wider than the front-to-back area to be covered. If necessary, carpet padding can be installed in multiple sections. Remember that the transmission hump, driveshaft tunnel, and depth of the floor pan in relation to the doorsill will have a significant impact on the actual width needed.

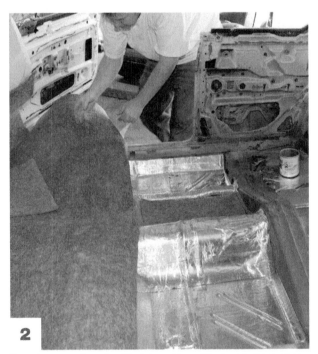

2 The main purpose of carpet padding is to provide a uniform base for the carpet. In an ideal situation, one layer under all of the carpet suffices, but most vehicle floor pans have various high and low spots, so carpet padding is used to smooth out those irregularities.

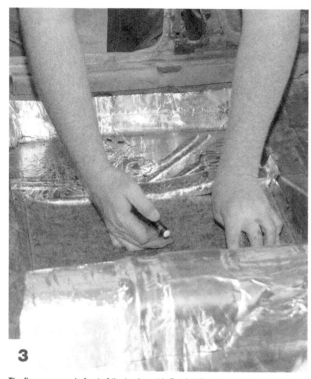

3

The floor pan area in front of the back seat is flat, but there is a raised panel in the floor above a sub-rail connector. Use one or two layers of carpet padding to even out any bumps in this area.

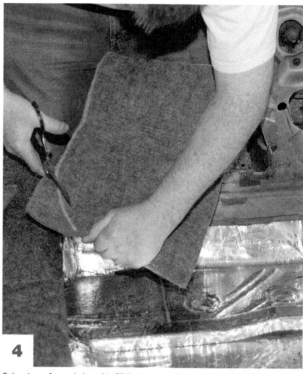

4

Cut a piece of carpet shaped to fill the low area. Cut rounded corners if necessary.

5

After trimming and verifying the correct fit of the carpet padding, apply spray adhesive to the face of the insulation material already in the vehicle and to the back of the carpet padding. The obstruction in the floor pan is more apparent in this photo.

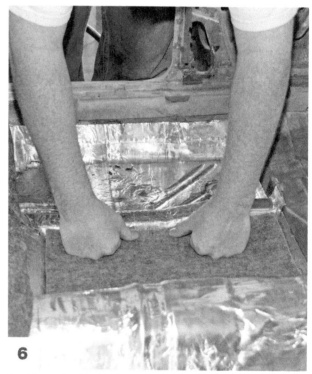

6

Press the carpet padding into place to ensure good contact between both surfaces. Glue the padding to avoid premature wear and tear, as the carpet moves around when anything rests upon it.

7

With one layer of carpet padding in place, it becomes apparent that multiple layers are required to completely level out the back seat floor pan area. The second layer is not required over the entire area, just a portion.

8

Continue gluing and laying padding until the bed is level.

9

Once the smaller pieces are secured and leveled, cover the entire area with a single piece of padding to provide a more uniform base for the carpet.

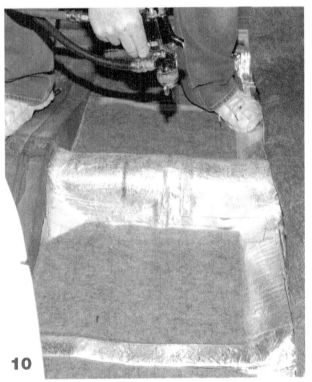

10

With the recesses of the rear floor pan filled in, install the overlying carpet padding. Use a spray gun to apply spray adhesive to the top of the last piece of filler padding and to the underside of the single piece of carpet padding.

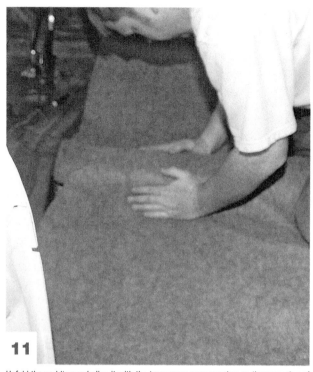

11

Unfold the padding and align it with the transverse crossmember on the rear edge of the carpeted area. Form the carpet padding to fit around the driveshaft tunnel, and press it into place on top of the driveshaft tunnel and all along the sides to where the floor becomes horizontal.

12

Once the rear portion of the padding is secured, spray adhesive on the driver-side insulation material and carpet padding.

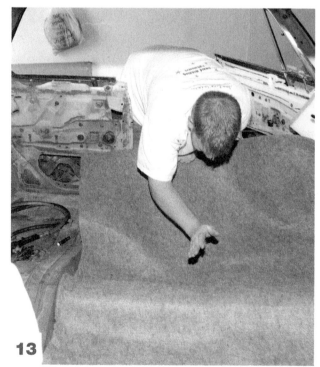

13

Work the driver-side padding into place, starting in the middle and moving outward. Hold the padding away from the adhesive with one hand and press it into place with the other hand.

14

With the front carpet padding glued in place, trim off any excess from the driver side. Begin at the back and press the carpet padding up against the vertical face of the transverse cross-member. Mark the intersection of the horizontal floor and the vertical wall.

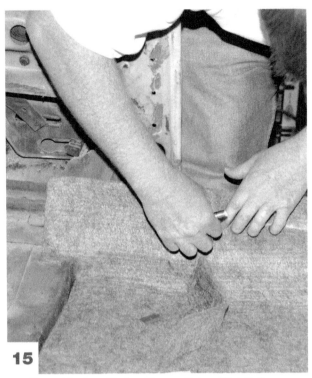

15

Trim off any padding beyond the line with a razor blade or utility knife, then move to the driver side and do the same. The weldment (aka pinch weld) around the door opening and under the weather stripping is a good place to start. Mark another chalk line and grab your shears.

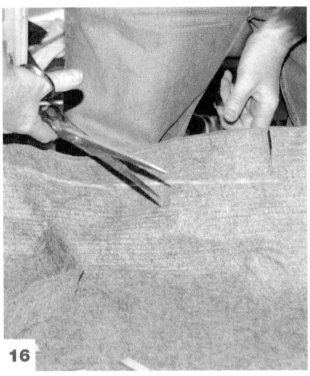

16

Cut the excess carpet. Leave enough padding to tuck under the doorsill plate, as that is what secures the carpet at the door opening.

17

After the rear half of the driver-side carpet padding is installed, move to the passenger side. Apply spray adhesive to the back of the carpet padding and the front side of the previous layers.

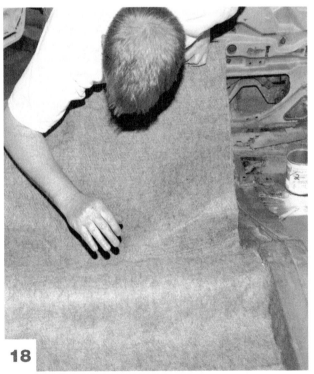

18

Hold the loose edge of the carpet padding up to avoid premature contact with the spray adhesive. Use your other hand to work the carpet padding down along the side of the driveshaft tunnel and across the floor.

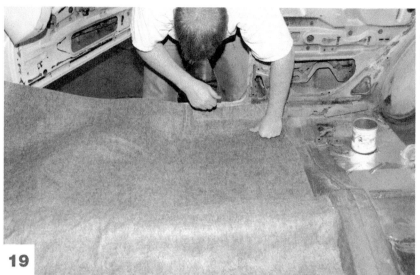

Press the padding flat across the floor and work it up along the short vertical wall that leads to the doorsill. To ensure that the spray adhesive does its job, firmly press the carpet padding down for good contact. Use a single-edged razor blade or utility knife to cut off any excess carpet at the back of the area, just as with the opposite side.

One piece of carpet padding often presents more problems than necessary, so cut a piece long enough to cover just beyond the point on the floor where the driveshaft tunnel and transmission hump flare out to provide more transmission room. Mark a straight line. Use a pair of shears to cut the carpet padding along its front edge.

Apply spray adhesive to the floor area and to the backside of the remaining loose carpet padding and unfold it into place.

Use a rubber mallet to press the carpet padding into place along the intersection of the driveshaft tunnel and the flat floor on both sides. Continue pressing the padding on the rest of the floor.

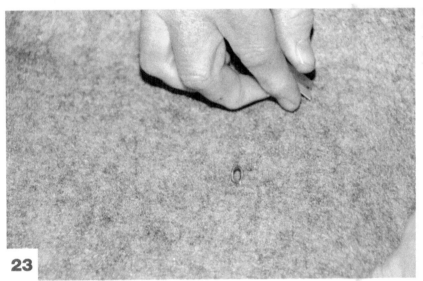

Before covering the rest of the floor, use fitting needles to probe through the carpet padding to find the holes in the floor pan for the bolts that secure the seats. When you find a hole, cut an opening in the carpet padding large enough for the mounting bolts to protrude through the floor.

Make a few alignment marks on both the carpet padding and the previously installed insulation. Since the transmission hump varies in shape, it forces the padding in different directions, making it essential to get the carpet centered from the start.

25

Apply spray adhesive on the entire transmission hump but not on the floor pans. Also apply spray adhesive to the corresponding back side of the middle portion of the carpet.

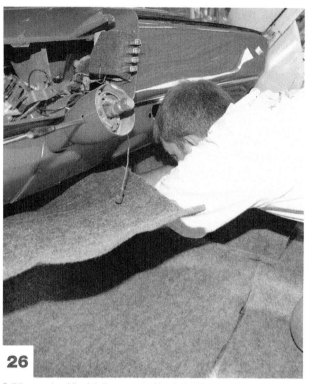

26

Roll the carpet padding into the proper position. It should abut the front edge of the previously installed carpet padding. Tuck the rest of the padding forward toward the firewall.

27

Make a heavy pass with spray adhesive where the two pieces of carpet padding meet. Notice that this seam of carpet padding is intentionally beneath where the seat will be located, making it less likely to tear due to foot traffic.

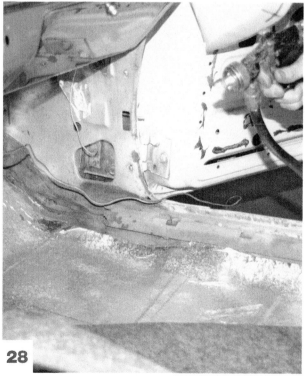

28

Apply spray adhesive to the rest of the front seat passenger floor area.

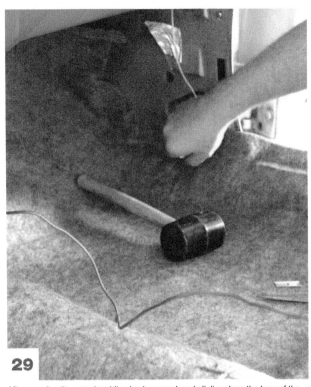

29

After pressing the carpet padding in place, mark a chalk line along the base of the pinch weld in the doorsill and the kick panel. Cut along this line with a pair of shears, and the passenger side is almost complete.

30

The driver side presents more challenges: a gas pedal, a brake pedal, a steering column, possibly an emergency brake pedal, and a dimmer switch. Address each of them individually as you work outward from the transmission hump.

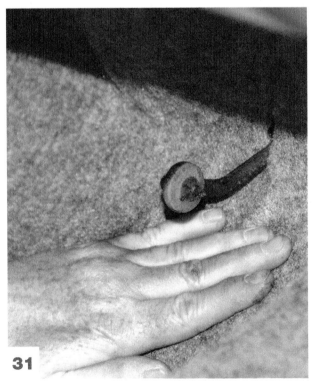

31

The gas pedal is first. Cut a slit in the carpet padding slightly wider than the width of this portion of the pedal. Slide the padding upward along both sides of the pedal. The same process is used to fit the carpet around the pedal.

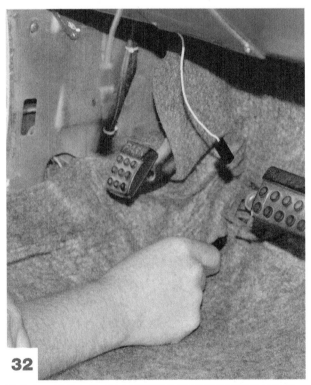

32

The brake pedal does not present a problem as it hangs from the master cylinder mounted on the firewall. If the brake pedal protrudes through the floor in the same way as the gas pedal, repeat the same process as for the gas pedal.

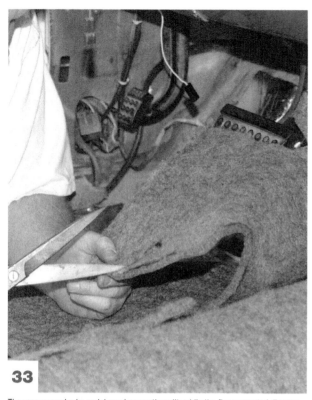

33

The emergency brake pedal requires another slit, while the floor-mounted dimmer switch is accessed with a hole cut in the carpet padding and the carpet. Carefully trim around the kick panel and doorsill.

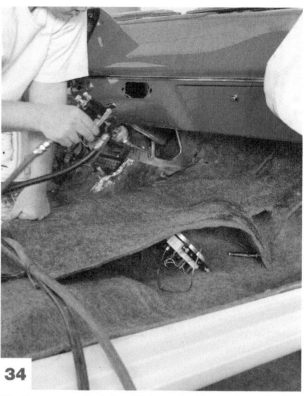

34

When the necessary cutting is done, fold the carpet padding face down and apply spray adhesive to its back.

35

Also apply spray adhesive to the previously installed insulation material.

36

Press the carpet padding into place. Install the carpet in much the same way.

Chapter 6
Headliners

For many people, the headliner in a vehicle is out of sight and out of mind. A headliner doesn't receive as much wear and tear as the seats or carpeting do, so people usually do not think about replacing it. However, since a headliner is affected by gravity, even the slightest bit of damage can cause the material to come loose. When a headliner starts pulling loose and sagging, it quickly detracts from the appearance of the vehicle. Replacing the headliner is not only an opportunity to increase the beauty of your vehicle, but also to add new insulation material to the roof, boosting the efficiency of the air conditioner.

Headliners come in three types, depending on the vehicle. Vehicles that were manufactured prior to World War II used structural supports to support a vinyl roof insert, because at that time the tooling wasn't available to make solid tops. These structural supports and the inside of the roof are usually covered with upholstery material stretched over top bows. Replacing this type of headliner is extremely labor intensive. Similar headliners are found in vehicles manufactured after World War II, but the roof is usually solid in the later models. On these vehicles, the inside of the roof material (vinyl or sheet metal) is seen from the passenger compartment if the headliner is not in place. In these models, damage to the roof quickly works its way to the interior.

The second type of headliner, in lower-priced vehicles and pickup trucks manufactured from the 1950s through the end of the 1990s, is actually no headliner at all. Double-wall construction allowed auto manufacturers to eliminate traditional headliners. The inside of the roof on many vehicles, as well as fiberglass reproductions of earlier vehicles, is usually smooth (although it may have character lines to provide support) and simply painted the same color as the rest of the interior of the vehicle. Rather than painting the entire expanse of sheet metal or fiberglass, many builders make good use of high-quality contact cement, lots of foam, and materials such as tweed or vinyl to make sculptured headliners. These headliners are usually constructed in similar fashion to a door panel and are attached to the inner roof panel with self-tapping sheet metal screws.

Late-model vehicles usually have a third type of headliner composed of a piece or pieces of formed material shaped to fit the inside of the roof. These headliners are covered with a variety of materials, ranging from the paltry to the plush. Similar technology is used to cover door pillars and other inside panels. These panels are held in place by other trim pieces, coat hooks, and passenger-assist handles. Replacing this type of headliner is usually just a matter of ordering a replacement from the dealer, removing the various trim pieces that secure the headliner, removing the headliner, and securing the replacement.

TRADITIONAL HEADLINERS

Headliners are made of lightweight material because they're not subject to daily abuse by being sat or pulled upon, although it's common to use the same material covering the seats for the headliner. Vinyl is a common choice for headliner material because it's durable, comes in a wide variety of colors, is relatively inexpensive, and is relatively lightweight when compared to mohair or leather.

Measuring

On many vehicles, the largest single upholstered panel is the headliner. Measure accurately; you'll need some extra material to stretch the headliner tight, and if you cut too small a piece, you won't have enough to cover the entire headliner. If measured incorrectly, a small piece of headliner can become a large piece of scrap.

An untrimmed headliner for a typical American four-door sedan might be close to 6 or 7 feet wide. A curved roof requires more material than a flat roof, and it is more difficult to measure a vehicle from the front to the back with a curved headliner. Measure from the front windshield along the actual location of the headliner and back to below the rear window all the way to the package tray. Add 12 to 18 inches to your measurement. Also measure side to side along the location of the headliner and then add about 1 foot. Also measure the spacing between the top bows.

Sketch a diagram of the headliner in the vehicle. Include any top bows and roof supports at their approximate locations. If the spacing between them varies, indicate that on the diagram.

Cutting

On a traditional headliner, several small strips are sewn together so that the seams run from side to side, instead of one large piece of material covering the ceiling of the vehicle. The material and seams are measured and cut so that they coincide with the top bows that span the vehicle from side to side. After you've sewn the pieces together to form one piece big enough to cover the entire area, fold the material in half to form a right side and a left side. Cut a small notch in each end of the material at the midpoint to use as a reference to ensure that the headliner is installed into the vehicle square.

Replacing or installing a custom headliner is one of the more subtle yet attractive custom upholstery projects.

PROJECT 9
Making and Installing a Traditional Headliner

Tools & Materials: Preferred cover material, measuring tape, sewing machine, listing, chalk or China marker, stapler, scissors, utility knife, straightedge, wind lace

Time: 2–4 hours

Skill Level: Basic

Cost: Low

Automobile manufactures could not stamp a complete roof out of sheet metal before the 1940s. So they used sheet metal for the perimeter of the roof, with a vast opening in the middle. They used vinyl to fill the gap. To support the flimsy roof, wooden (usually oak or another hardwood) top bows were cut to size. They spanned the roof from side to side, spaced approximately 8 to 14 inches apart. Listing was sewn to the back of the headliner material and secured to the top bows. For a firsthand look at how this was done, follow along as Jerry Klitch installs a headliner in a Model A Ford coupe. A similar process is used in a sedan. The only real difference is the number of pieces of material sewn together and the number of top bows.

1 This Model A coupe has a filled roof, meaning that a piece of sheet metal has been welded in place to cover the hole that was originally filled with a vinyl insert. Even with the filled roof, the wooden top bows provide structural support to the upper body.

2 A coupe has only five top bows, while a sedan has more. In either case, the headliner is secured with the top bows. The headliner is secured to the front of the top bows if you start in the back and work your way forward, or to the rear if you start in the front and work toward the back.

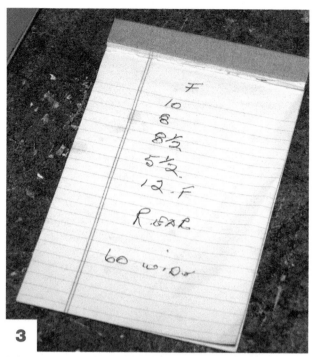

3

Before cutting any material, measure the overall width and the spacing between the top bows, writing down the measurements for future reference. You cannot easily measure the length of the top bows because they may be different widths, and material is secured to the front or back but not to the face of the wood. On this Model A, none of the distances are the same. Precise measurements are crucial.

4

Cut the covering material into 60-inch strips, with each strip the same width as you found the center bows to be. Sew the covering pieces together in the same order as the bows, or the headliner will not match the layout.

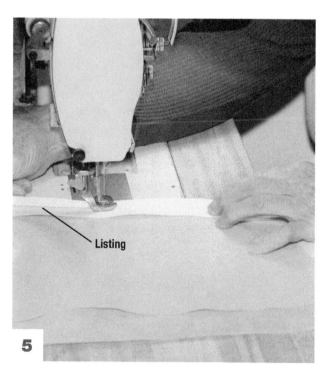

5

In addition to sewing the multiple pieces of material together, sew a listing (sold in rolls for this purpose) to the back of each seam. The listing serves as a vertical tab to secure to the front or back edge of the wooden top bow, allowing the headliner material to remain flat in the horizontal position.

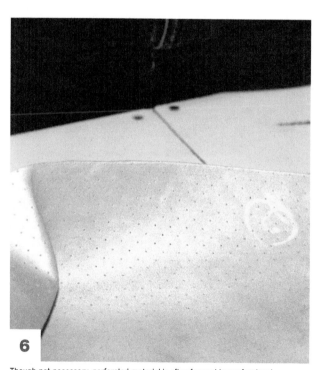

6

Though not necessary, perforated material is often favored by professional upholsterers because it not only makes the material noticeably lighter, but also allows it to breathe and more easily adjust to ambient temperatures. No matter which kind of material you use, number each piece of material with chalk.

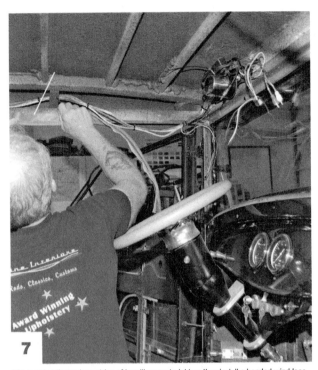

7 After sewing the various strips of headliner material together, install a beaded wind lace around the top of the door openings. Wind lace is made by wrapping a piece of cord or piping with a piece of material and stitching along the edge of the cord. Tack or staple the remaining wind lace material to the wooden structure surrounding the door opening.

8 After the wind lace is installed, only the beaded portion is seen. The headliner covers the flat portion. Get the wind lace as straight as possible. Secure it with a tack or a staple about every inch. Do not pinch or pierce any wires in the area.

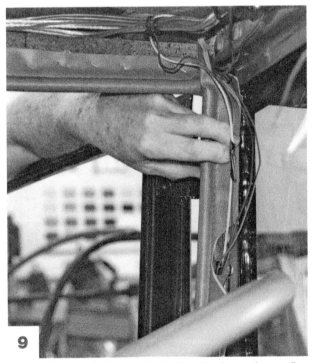

9 Wind lace must be installed along the front and back of the door opening, as well as the top. Wiring from beneath the dash is routed upward through the body's A-pillar to the outside of the face. It continues upward to the stereo and the windshield wiper motor above the windshield. Notch the wind lace for wiring, as it will be later covered with a garnish molding.

10 The wind lace continues all the way down to the floor on both sides of the door opening. With the wooden structure of the Model A, it is easy to secure the wind lace in place.

11

With the wind lace installed along both doors, reinstall the dash rail (a trim piece that fits at the top of the dash). Eventually, a vertical garnish molding will be installed to cover the inside of the body's A-pillar.

12

Measure to find the horizontal center of the top of the front top bow. Also measure to find the center of the rearmost top bow.

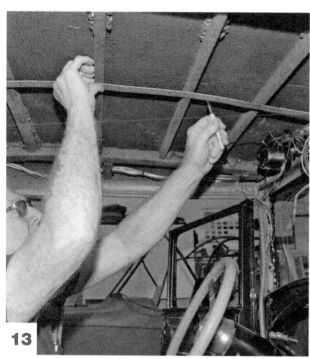

13

Using a flexible straightedge and a permanent marker, mark the center on each of the top bows by connecting the front and rear dots. Because the center of each listing has already been marked or notched, align the center of the headliner and the center of each top bow. Make thick and precise marks; it is essential that the headliner is properly aligned. A short misalignment on a smaller coupe might not be noticeable or cause much stress, but on a longer sedan, the error will be significantly more pronounced.

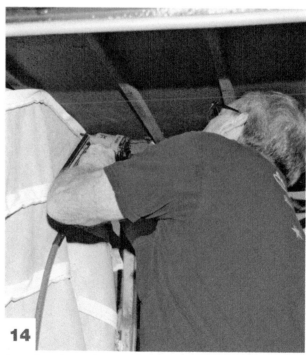

14

Jerry prefers to begin in the back of the vehicle and work forward, so the listing will be secured to the front edge of each top bow. Align the center notch of the first seam of the headliner material with the center mark of the first top bow and staple the headliner in place. Work to one side along the same bow all the way to one end. Work from the center to the opposite side, installing staples approximately every 1/2 inch.

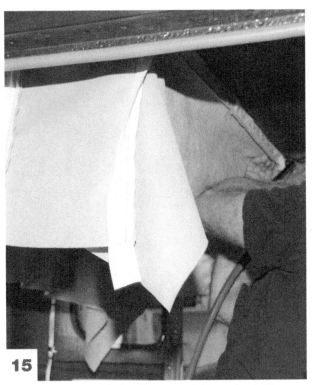

15

Repeat the process at each top bow. The excess material on each end will be trimmed off later.

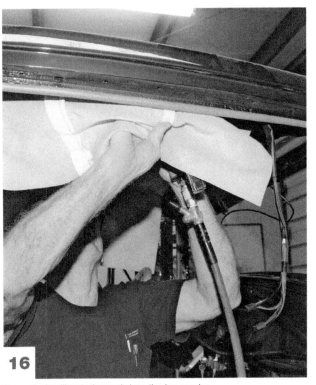

16

Secure the headliner to the wood above the door opening.

17

At this point, the headliner is completely stapled into position. Trimming off the excess and installing the overhead console are all that remain.

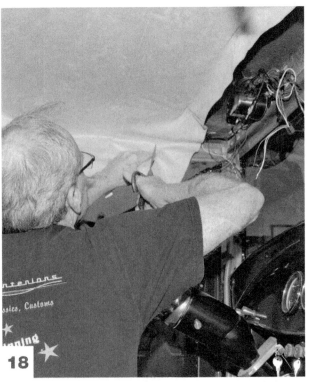

18

The very front of the interior roof area will be covered by an overhead console, so the headliner will not extend past the front top bow. In this photo, Jerry is cutting material from around a metal bracket designed to support the overhead console. The bracket itself is secured to the wood above the door.

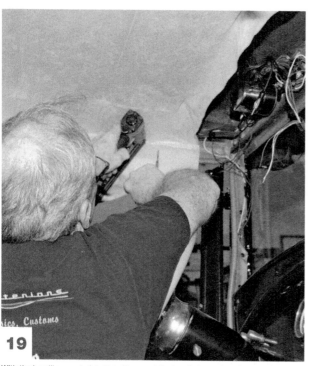

19

With the headliner material slit to fit around the bracket mentioned in the previous caption, staple it in place above the top of the door.

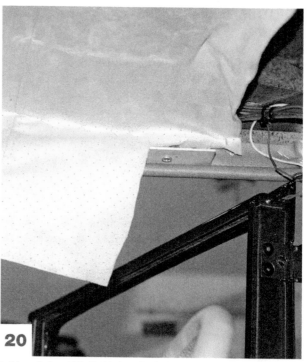

20

In this particular vehicle, the interior walls of the entire body are going to be covered with upholstery material, so another piece of wind lace will eventually cover the seam between the horizontal covering of the headliner and vertical covering of the interior wall. You could also install the headliner and the wind lace around the doors to cover the edge of the headliner.

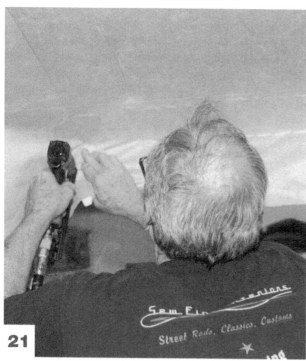

21

Install a row of staples to secure the headliner to a piece of wood that runs front to back along the corner formed by the roof and the interior body panels. Excess material is cut just slightly below the row of staples. This edge will be covered by wind lace and upholstery material, similar to the interior wall panels.

22

Lift and secure the overhead compartments into place. A stereo head unit will eventually be placed into the large opening of the console where the wires are visible. The two switches are for the power windows. The opening at the right is a small compartment for a garage door opener or other small gadget.

SCULPTURED HEADLINERS

Manufacturers can now stamp sheet metal into areas as large as roof panels. With this ability, and with the use of inner and outer body panels, traditional headliners have disappeared from contemporary vehicles. But that does not mean you are stuck with a painted interior roof panel. With the improvements in spray-on adhesives, it is easier than ever to make a custom headliner with a pattern without lifting a needle. You may want to continue any patterns already found on door panels or use a simple geometric design. Making a sculptured headliner is much like making a sculptured door panel.

The first step is to determine the size and shape of the area to be covered. Then use a piece of pattern paper (approximately 1/16-inch-thick tag board) and cut a pattern the same size and shape as the area to be covered. Mark mounting holes for sun visors or dome lights on the pattern. After all potential obstacles are accounted for, mark the locations for screws to attach the headliner to the roof of the vehicle. Secure the panel to the roof with no. 8 self-tapping sheet metal screws that are long enough to go through the material, padding, and panel board but not long enough to cause damage to the vehicle's roof. Sketch the design onto pattern paper.

With the design finalized, cut any designed portions from the pattern paper and lay it onto panel board. Just as with custom door panels, use luaun plywood or preformed ABS panels approximately 1/8 inch thick. Transfer the pattern onto the panel board by tracing around it with chalk. Since the panel will be multilayered, use alignment holes to make sure the pattern lines up correctly. Drill at least two holes in each layer of panel board that align with holes in the previous layer. The alignment holes should be between 1/16 and 1/8 inch in diameter and just slightly larger than whatever you are using for alignment pins.

Cut a piece of closed-cell foam slightly larger than the panel board. Spray the back of the foam and the front of the panel board with spray adhesive. Lay the board face down onto the foam and press the two together so they make good contact. Flip both pieces over and use a roller to eliminate any air bubbles, working from the middle toward the edges.

Trim off any excess foam with a razor blade or utility knife. Smooth the edges of the panel board with 80- to 120-grit sandpaper. Closed-cell foam has a slick surface; use a sanding block with 80- to 120-grit sandpaper to roughen it and to provide superior adhesion for subsequent layers of foam. Use the design pattern and cut another piece of closed-cell foam. Trace the outline of the pattern onto the foam-covered panel board with a piece of chalk. Apply spray adhesive to both surfaces and position the second piece of closed-cell foam onto the panel, using the alignment holes for position. Press the foam firmly into place, making sure that positioning is correct and that bubbles are eliminated.

After all the necessary layers have been glued into place, it is time to cut the upholstery material. Unroll the material, place the panel board onto it, and cut the material slightly oversize. Apply spray adhesive to approximately half of the back of the material and to the corresponding portion of the front of the panel to be covered. With the panel board face-up, position the upholstery material upon it, making sure that excess material falls on all sides.

Begin pressing the material into the three-dimensional design you created with the layers of closed-cell foam. Use a small roller for intricate patterns. Start near the center of the area where adhesive has been applied and work your way out toward the edges. As you get closer to the remaining half of the panel, spray adhesive on the back of the remaining upholstery material and the face of the panel board and continue pressing the material into place. Large, flowing patterns are easier to work with than small, intricate designs. With the material pressed into place around all the design elements, press the flat portion into place with a large roller.

When the entire front portion of the panel has been pressed into place, flip the panel over and spray adhesive around the edge of it and onto about 1 inch of the excess material. Wrap the material around the edge onto the back of the panel. Use a single-edged razor blade to cut off the excess, leaving approximately 1 inch of material on the back of the panel board.

Install the finished headliner by threading self-tapping screws through the panel board into the inside layer of the double wall of the roof. Reinstall the sun visors, dome lights, and passenger-assist handles to secure the panel in place.

PROJECT 10
Covering a Simple Overhead Console

 Time: 2–4 hours

 Skill Level: Basic

 Cost: Low

 Tools & Materials: Utility knife, shears, awl or leather punch, spray adhesive, sewing machine and thread, closed-cell foam padding (optional), preferred cover material

Like the rest of the Model A, the car's sheet metal console is pretty simple. Whether a console is simple or complicated, the process for covering one is the same. You cover the console with the desired material, securing it to the face and wrapping it around the back as well. You cut openings for switches, stereo speakers, and so on and then install the accessories and the console. Follow along as Jerry Klitch shows just how easy it is to cover an owner-fabricated overhead console. (This project does not include a layer of closed-cell foam, which is more appropriate on newer vehicles.)

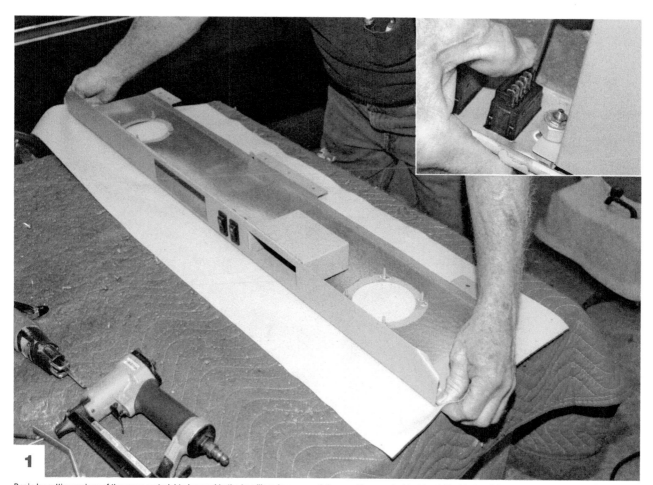

1 Begin by cutting a piece of the same material to be used in the headliner, large enough to cover the console (vinyl here). Electrical switches need to be removed before the console can be covered (inset). Be sure to note which switch goes where, which way it is oriented, and what it should be reconnected to.

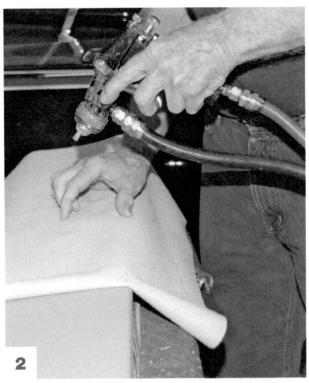

2

After positioning the vinyl material on the console, fold back about half of it. Apply spray adhesive to the back of the material and to the face of the console.

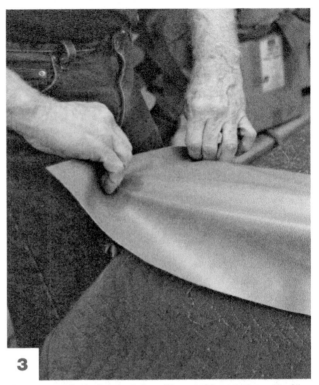

3

After the spray adhesive becomes tacky, pull the material over the lower side of the console, pressing out any wrinkles in the process. Press the material in place over the edge and front faces of the console. Holes for switches and the like will be cut in the vinyl later.

4

With half the console covered, apply spray adhesive to the back of the remaining material and to the bottom and front face of the console.

5

Pull the vinyl taut over the bottom of the console and press it into place.

6

Press the vinyl over the flat edge of the console and the mounting brackets.

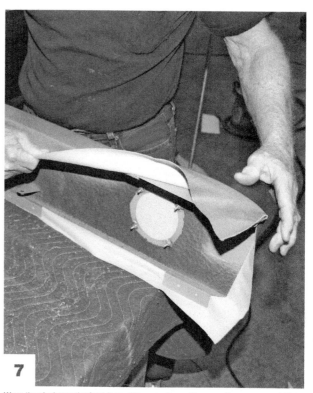

7

Wrap the vinyl over the front face of the console, making sure there are no wrinkles and that the vinyl is taut.

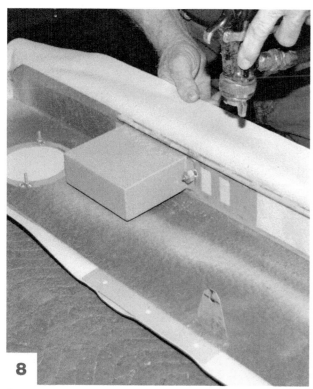

8

Spray adhesive onto the inside edges of the console and the corresponding portions of the vinyl.

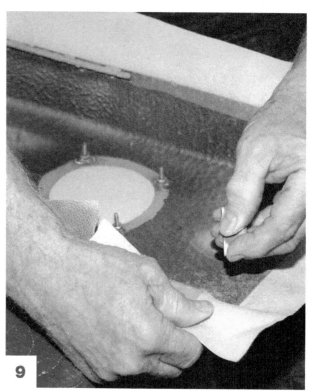

9

While waiting for the adhesive to become tacky, use a single-edged razor blade or utility knife to trim the short sections of excess vinyl from around the mounting brackets on the leading edge of the console.

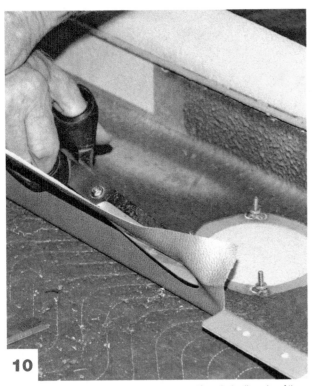

10

Use shears to trim the longer sections of excess vinyl from the leading edge of the console. After trimming the vinyl, wrap the remaining material around the edge of the console.

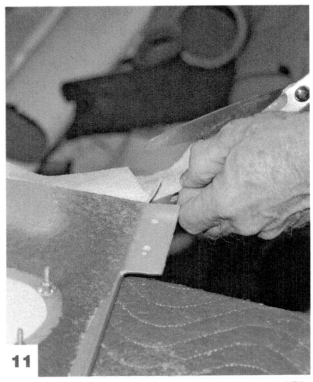

11

At each end of the console, make an approximately 45-degree cut on the vinyl. This will let the vinyl cover the complete edge of the sheet metal while still easily folding over to the back of the metal.

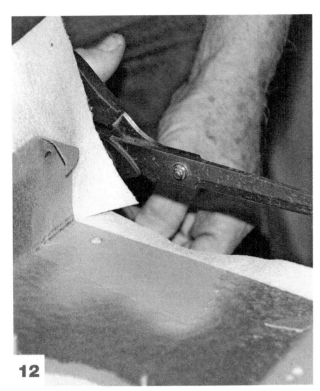

12

Cut the vinyl so that approximately 1 inch remains to be wrapped around to the back of the sheet metal console. Apply spray adhesive to the inside of the 1-inch tab, fold the tab over, and press it into place.

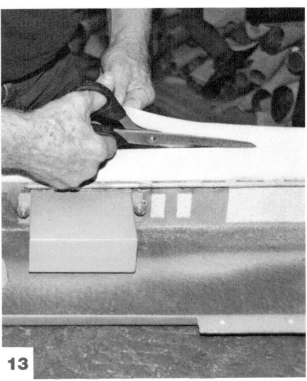

13

Trim the excess material from the front (short) face of the console with a pair of shears.

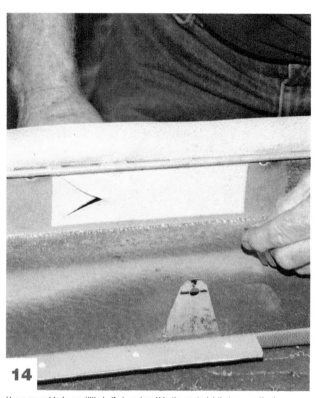

14

Use a razor blade or utility knife to cut an X in the material that covers the large opening for the stereo head unit.

15

Trim a 45-degree bevel on each flap of vinyl and fold the flaps over, pressing them into place on the back of the sheet metal. Trim excess vinyl around each opening with a singled-edged razor blade or utility knife.

16

On the opposite end of the console, trim the material just enough to cover the edges. Trim away any excess.

17

With the vinyl folded over and pressed into place, the end of the console is now covered.

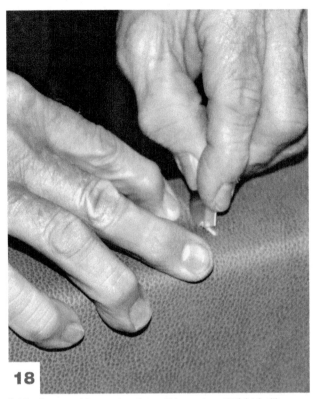

18

Cut the three remaining openings (two switches and one stash box) with an X pattern.

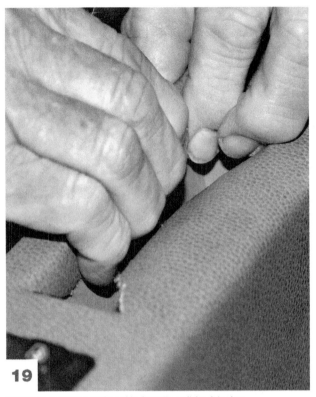

19

Fold the vinyl over toward the inside. Press the switches into place.

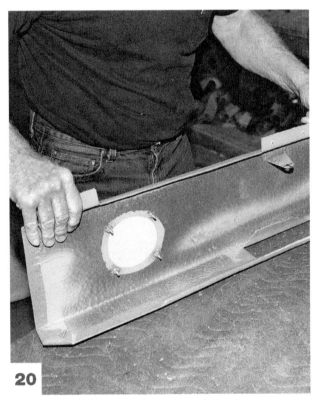

20

All that is left to do is punch holes in the speaker openings.

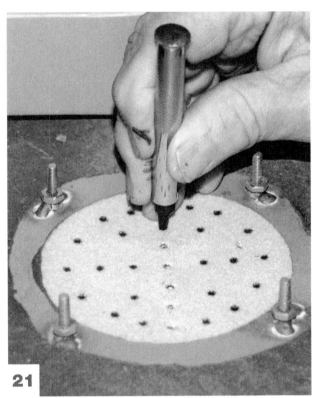

21

Mark the positions of each hole on the back of the vinyl, and use a leather punch to make the holes.

Chapter 7
Secondary Interior Areas

In the design stages of an automotive interior restoration, always keep the vehicle's functionality in mind. Owners shouldn't have to completely remove upholstered components to do routine maintenance. If a serviceable component is hidden behind an upholstered panel, make it easy to remove that panel. With snaps or hooks and loops, you should be able to make most anything accessible. For instance, a fuse panel can be hidden behind an easily removed upholstered panel.

In many hot rods, the master cylinder is below the floor. If this is the case on your vehicle, consider using a remote reservoir, which allows the driver to check and fill the brake master cylinder without having to remove carpet or another interior floor covering.

Whenever you are building a custom vehicle or making significant changes to a stock configuration, do yourself a favor and sit in the vehicle prior to completing the interior. You may find that mounting the seat forward, backward, higher, or lower provides better seating.

The rear portion of the console is styled to closely match the contour of the seats. It also houses speakers for the stereo.

PROJECT 11
Building a Center Console

 Time: 2–4 hours

 Skill Level: Basic

 Cost: Low

 Tools & Materials: Pattern board, MDF, masking tape, straightedge, radius template, pencil or light marker, shears, scroll saw, drywall screws, electric drill, scrap wood spacers, pneumatic stapler, staples

A center console can serve as a mounting location for stereo equipment, various vehicle controls, cup holders, or as hidden storage. It can be finished in a variety of ways: completely covered with upholstery material, completely painted, or a combination of the two. Crafting a center console requires a certain amount of skill in fabrication and design, but the process is not overly complicated. With a basic understanding of how to construct a console, the only limiting factor is your imagination. Here, Brian Flynn of Sew Fine Interiors begins work.

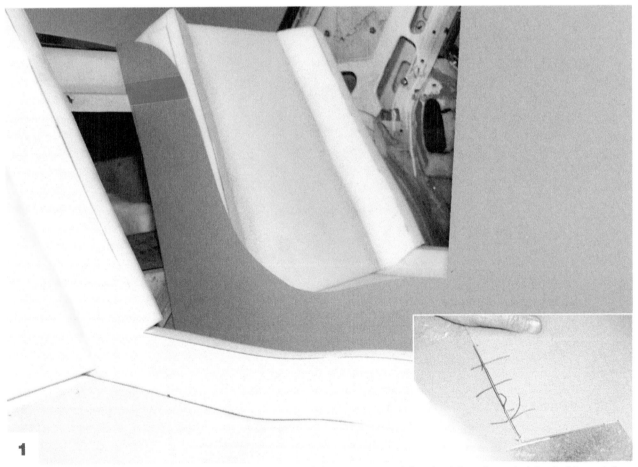

1

Starting with pieces of pattern board, Brian establishes the profile of the center console. In this case, the console flows from between the rear bucket seats all the way to the dash. Cut the bottom of the pattern board to fit the contour of the vehicle's floor pan and the top of the board to match the desired profile. Since pattern board is available in limited sizes, multiple pieces will need to be spliced together for a full-length console. It is OK to overlap the pattern board by an inch or so. Mark some lines across both pieces at the seam so that the pieces are properly aligned (inset).

2

Use several pieces of masking tape to tape the two pieces of pattern board together.

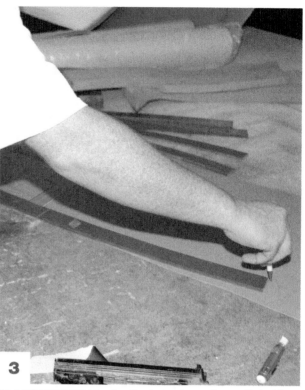

3

Use a radius template to trace along the edge to get a smooth curve. Much of the layout will be trial and error. There is no true right or wrong layout.

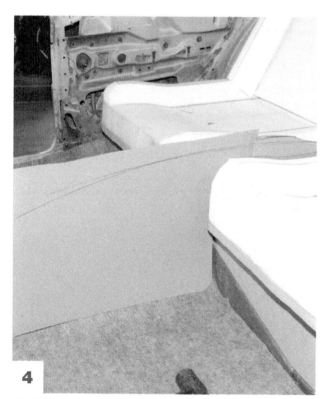

4

This design will separate the floor pan between each rear-seat passenger. It could be lower or higher, depending on the desired effect. As it flows forward, it will travel downward between the two front bucket seats.

5

The blue bucket seat will be recovered eventually, but for now it serves to determine the best profile for the console. Except for cuts to allow the pattern to match the floor pan, the profile is not cut out until the full length is drawn.

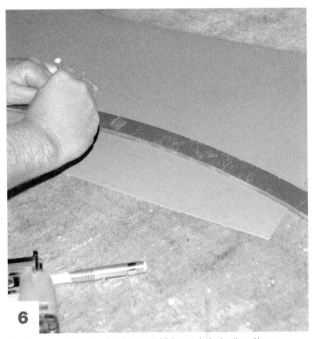

6

By using composite radius templates, establish your desired pattern. Here, a smooth, roller-coaster-type profile is sketched.

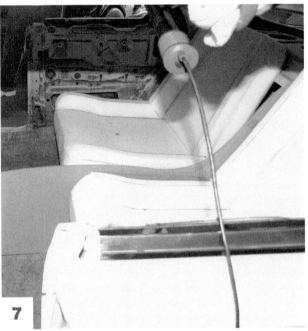

7

From this photo, we can see how the bulk of the pattern is made. The pattern provides a slight armrest between the rear passengers, as well as a potential mounting point for rear stereo speakers in the vertical portion between the seats. The high area between the front and rear seats could also include cup holders, rear A/C and heat controls (and vents), or even a DVD player. Although the pattern is not complete, Brian has planned ahead. He has the middle portion sweeping into an upward curve that will eventually meet the dash.

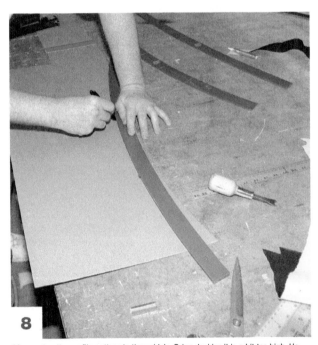

8

After seeing the profile pattern in the vehicle, Brian decides it is a bit too high. He makes some reference marks to indicate how much lower the profile needs to be, since will it not necessarily be an even reduction in height. Then, using the radius templates, he draws some lines to bring the profile roughly 3 inches lower at most and slightly less at some points. Regardless, the profile will end up with a smooth curve.

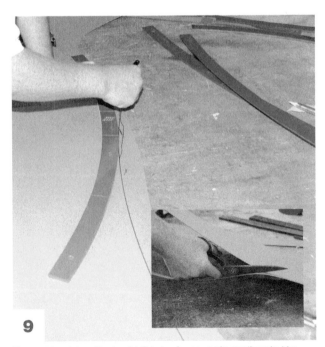

9

The curve templates will not match Brian's reference marks exactly, so he tries curves of different radii to see what looks best. Use a pencil or a light marker while tracing the initial curves. Use a heavier marker to delineate the final cut. When the revised profile is established, cut the pattern board with a pair of shears (inset).

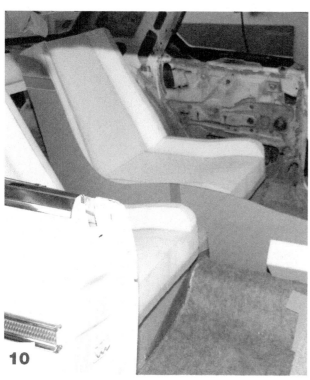

10

The revised profile provides a lower, sleeker, and perhaps more pleasing design. The white rectangle on the right of the photo is simply a chunk of foam used to prop up the pattern.

11

Brian concentrates on the fit with the vehicle's dash. He starts with a small piece of scrap pattern board cut to fit the outline of the dash and long enough to be spliced to the rest of the pattern.

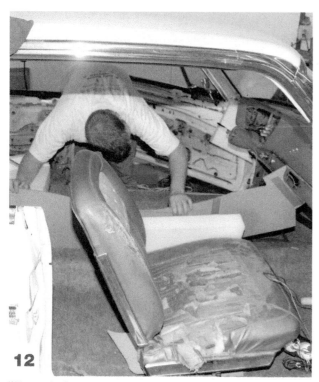

12

With a couple of splices made, the pattern is almost complete. Since it runs from the dash to the back of the passenger compartment, there is still some work to do. The finished profile needs to be established at the dash, and a filler panel needs to be made to fill the gap between the bottom of the pattern and the floor pan.

13

Modify the upper profile by adding a smooth radius leading into a more vertical transition to the bottom of the dash. As evidenced by blue tape near the bottom of the pattern board, a filler panel has been added between the bottom of the pattern and the floor.

14

Lay out the finished pattern on a piece of MDF, which will be used to construct one side of the center console. Cut out a second piece using the same template to make the other side. Hold the pattern in place with one hand and trace it with the other without moving the pattern; you might need a couple of clamps to keep the whole pattern steady.

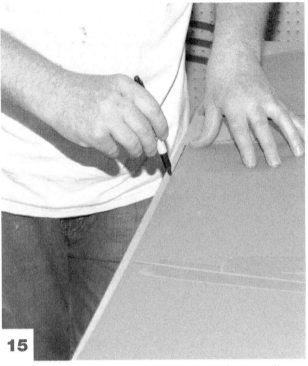

15

Note that a sliver of MDF needs to be removed at the bottom of the pattern. You cannot assume that the floor is going to be perfectly flat. Multiple pieces of MDF are required for this particular pattern.

16

Using a scroll saw, begin cutting the MDF along the pattern line. The smoother the pattern, the more accurately it can be cut. The more accurately you follow the pattern line, the less follow-up work is required.

17

Check the fit of the MDF console side one last time prior to cutting out the other side. What looks like a gap just below the stock radio opening in the dash is actually a shadow. If you look close, you can see that the MDF fits the dash outline quite nicely.

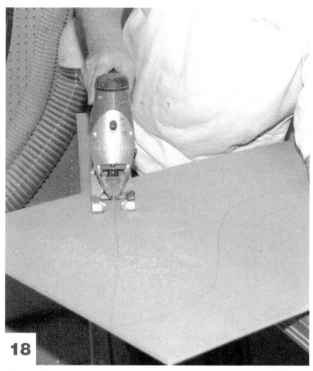

18

After checking the first side for proper fit and tracing the pattern onto additional sheets of MDF, begin cutting out the second side of the console.

19

Scrap pieces of MDF and drywall screws are used to splice the console sides together. The side panels abut each other; a scrap piece of MDF is secured to both pieces with multiple drywall screws. Remember that the outside of the console panel must remain as smooth as possible.

20

In addition to splicing the side panels together, 2x4 wood scraps are used to separate the side panels. Three or four drywall screws installed through the MDF into each end of the 2x4s adequately secure it.

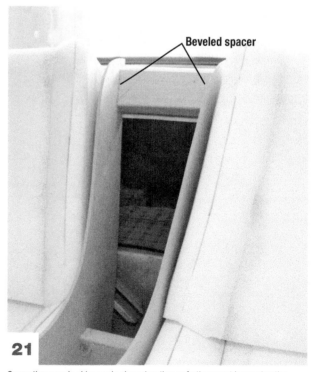

Beveled spacer

21

Space the console side panels closer together or farther apart by varying the position of the 2x4s. Note that in situations such as this, where the top of the console flares out to more closely match the outline of the seats, the wooden spacer block needs to be beveled to the correct angle.

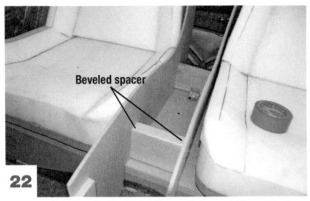

22

Use spacer blocks throughout the length of the console to prevent it from caving in on itself. Cut and bevel the blocks so that the side panels fit squarely against them.

23

Fabricate the top of the console after the full length of the console is spliced together and adequately spaced. Cut the top from 1/8- or 1/4-inch-thick MDF, which will be fairly flexible. Cut a strip wide enough to fit over the widest portion of the console and long enough to fit the full length. It may be necessary to splice multiple pieces together for the full length. Attach the top with staples and a pneumatic stapler Cut off any excess with a scroll saw.

Conflicting work schedules did not allow me to photograph the finished console, but it could have been finished in multiple methods, limited only by your imagination. The sides could have been covered with floor carpeting and the top with the same material used to cover the seats. A variation is to cover the entire console with the same material as the seats. The decision might depend on how much the vehicle will actually be driven versus how much it will be a show vehicle. Another variation is to paint a portion of the console or the entire unit, which requires using fiberglass or plastic body filler to create a paintable surface.

Prior to any finishing work, cut the necessary holes for mounting stereo speakers, courtesy lights, cup holders, electrical switches, or anything else that will be integrated into the console. The following photographs do not cover the entire scope of possibilities for a center console but should provide you with some inspiration.

This console serves as a mounting location for a variety of equipment. Just below the stock dash are the ignition switch and a knob (probably for headlights). Below them are the HVAC control panel, a built-in GPS or possibly a control for pneumatic ride height, and what I believe is a remote control for stereo system. On each side is a courtesy light.

This console is very simple and blends in nicely with the rest of the interior. It serves as a mounting location for the stereo/GPS, three control knobs, and a storage area between the seats. Notice how a piece of chrome or stainless-steel trim serves as a handle for the storage area.

Whenever you completely reupholster a vehicle, anything you neglect to touch is going to look worse than it did before and may even detract from your work. You may not be interested in touching up interior accessories, but they contribute to the overall look and feel of a custom interior. After all, you want to showcase the car in the best possible light. Details matter.

The Dash

In OEM vehicles, the dash is typically finished in one of three ways: fully painted, fully padded with a cover, or a combination of the two. Most vehicles built prior to the 1960s had a painted dash decorated with various amounts of chrome or stainless-steel trim, depending on the vehicle. As safety became more of an issue, manufacturers began using dashes that were padded and covered with vinyl. Some dashes were completely covered. Others were padded on top and painted beneath.

Most interior paint is the same as exterior paint, with the addition of a flattening agent to provide a semiflat appearance. For late-model vehicles, an auto body and paint supply store can decipher the paint code of your vehicle and provide an exact match for the interior paint. For custom colors (non-OEM), ask the counter person to add flattening agent to the paint purchased for the interior, as a premixed paint with flattening agent is probably not available. Try some paint on an inconspicuous spot and judge your results—this is a trial-and-error application. As the flattening agent cannot be removed from the paint, it is better to try a small amount and then add more flattener as desired. However, most upholstery shops do not perform any paint work, even though many interior surfaces are indeed painted, so be sure to review your custom project start-to-finish with your local upholstery shop to fully understand all your options and restrictions.

If the vehicle is equipped with an OEM dash pad, the pad might be faded, cracked, or peeling. Dash pads are usually held in place with small screws, some of which are easy to find and some more difficult. Screws are commonly found on the underside of the dash, along the lower front edge, and near the windshield. You may need to remove stereo speaker grilles and defrost outlets or open the glove box door to find all the screws. Consult a collision repair manual for the vehicle if you can't find them all. Once you have removed all the screws that secure the dash pad in place, it should lift right up off the dash.

Replacement dash pads for most vehicles are available through a variety of sources. Depending on the popularity of your vehicle, you might be able to find the exact color dash pad that came with it or one that matches the new upholstery. You can also purchase paint specifically designed for interior vinyl products from an automotive paint and supply store. Some interior paints require primers; ask the sales rep what is required when you purchase your paint.

Wash the dash pad with warm soapy water to remove any dirt, grease, or other contaminants that might present adhesion problems. Allow the dash pad to thoroughly dry and then apply the proper primer (if necessary). Once the primer has dried, apply the color coats as instructed. When the dash pad has completely dried, lay it in place on top of the dash and secure it with screws. You might want to spend a few extra dollars and buy an interior trim screw set so that old, grungy, greasy screws don't distract from your new interior.

Just because a dash has been previously painted does not mean that it cannot be upholstered. Any removable dash can be upholstered. If the shape of the dash includes compound curves, trying to cover it with material may cause bubbles. If you're using stainless-steel or aluminum trim on the dash, you might be able to force the bubbles to a trim-covered area and slice the material to let the bubbles escape. After removing all the gauges, stereo components, and heat and A/C controls, remove the dash from the vehicle. Remember that openings for these components will need to be enlarged by the thickness of the foam padding and the upholstery material *prior* to installing the foam padding.

Prior to covering the dash, add a layer of padding. Cut out a piece of 3/16- or 1/4-inch-thick closed-cell foam big enough to cover the entire dash. Splice pieces of the padding if necessary. Apply plenty of spray adhesive near any seams and butt the pieces of padding so there are no visible gaps or overlap. Fold half of the foam over on itself and spray the back with spray adhesive. Then spray the top of the dash with spray adhesive. Tape masking paper over the windshield if the dash doesn't have to be removed. When the spray adhesive is tacky, lay the foam onto the dash, making sure it overlaps the dash in all directions. Use your fingers or a small roller to work the foam into any low spots in the dash and to press the foam firmly into place. Apply spray adhesive to the back of the rest of the foam and the front of the dash, allow the adhesive to become tacky, and finish covering the dash with foam padding. Trim off any excess padding with a razor knife. Use a razor knife to cut away excess padding from any openings in the dash.

Upholstery material is installed in the same manner. Cut out a piece large enough to cover the entire dash, allowing for some overlap around all the edges. Just as with the padding, fold half the material over on itself. Spray the back of the material and the top of the foam padding on the dash with spray adhesive and then press the material into place, pressing out any bubbles or wrinkles as you go. Spray adhesive onto the back of the remaining material and the front of the dash. Then smooth the rest of the material into place.

At openings in the dash, use a razor knife to cut small slits into the material, so it can be pressed back into the opening. If the opening is not large enough to accommodate a small piece of folded material, use an ice pick or an awl to poke a hole in the upholstery material. From the back of the dash, apply spray adhesive to the dash and to the back of the material protruding from the front of the dash. Press the tabs of material onto the back of the dash, making sure the edges of the openings are covered. Trim off excess material except for about 1 inch all the way around the dash. Apply spray adhesive to this material and to the back of the dash and press the material into place, covering all the edges. You may now reinstall the dash and all its components.

Steering Column/Wheel

With all the new upholstery around the steering column and steering wheel, they may not look quite as good as they did before. You could paint the steering column while it's in place, but it is much easier to remove it from the vehicle than to do all the necessary masking. The steering column is typically connected to the vehicle at three locations: where the column passes through or under the dash, where it passes through the floor or firewall, and where it connects to the steering box or steering shafts. Refer to the manufacturer's instructions on how to remove the steering column.

On many custom vehicles, people use chrome or polished aluminum steering columns instead of repainting the column the original color. Custom columns add some sparkle to an area that is typically plush but not shiny, making an otherwise boring item a flashy highlight in the interior. Of course, most people spare the expense of a chrome steering column on the family sedan.

If you decide to keep the current steering column (whether you repaint it or not), you can easily add a new steering wheel to update the look of the interior. Steering wheels are available at automotive swap meets from $20 all the way up to $400 and more. Depending on the type of steering wheel purchased and the steering column in the vehicle, you might have to buy an adaptor to make the two components work together. Adaptors are typically available from vendors that sell custom parts.

If the existing steering wheel is cracked or broken, you can buy a kit to repair it. Steering wheel repair kits are advertised in many restoration magazines and in *Hemmings Motor News*.

Dome Lights

Other than replacing a damaged lens, chances are you won't customize or detail a dome light or any other interior lights. The dome light lens usually snaps into place or is secured by a couple screws, so while you are detailing your new interior, it doesn't take much to remove the lens and clean it well. When was the last time you did that? Soap, water, and a little scrubbing with a soft brush will work wonders. If the bezel is chrome, stainless steel, or aluminum, clean it with chrome polish and a soft cloth.

If your vehicle does not have a dome light, a great time to add or replace one is prior to installing a new headliner. Of course, if the existing light doesn't work, replace the bulb before you replace the light fixture itself. A dome light needs a wire to a power source such as the fuse panel and a method of obtaining a ground (either through a wire to a ground or in the mounting of the light fixture itself). Depending on the vehicle and how it is wired, the dome light needs to be switched on manually, turned on with the headlight switch, or activated whenever the doors are opened.

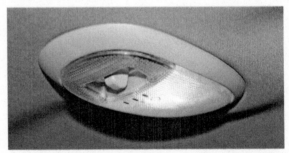

A functional domelight is a valuable amenity, no matter the era of vehicle.

Mirrors

While a rearview mirror is never the focal point of a vehicle's interior, it shouldn't be overlooked. Even a chrome-plated mirror outlined in flames will look better than a forty-year-old factory mirror with factory paint bubbling and peeling off it.

In older vehicles, the rearview mirror is usually mounted on a pedestal that hangs from above the windshield and is held in place by two or three screws. In newer vehicles, the mirror is usually mounted on a bracket glued to the inside of the windshield. Either type is easy to remove and can be cleaned with soap and water.

Depending on the color of your vehicle and your new upholstery, you may want to paint the mirror housing. To do so, remove the mirror from the vehicle, clean it with soap and water, mask off the glass, and paint it the color of your choice. If you have recently painted your vehicle (inside or out) you may have enough leftover paint for the job. A touchup gun or airbrush works great when painting something this size, as not much paint is required. If you don't have a spray gun or don't feel the need to match the color, a spray can of a neutral color paint works fine.

Sun Visors

A typical sun visor consists of three major components: the visor mounting bracket, the visor flap, and the optional upholstery. The mounting bracket is a metal rod with a slight bend in the middle. It is usually attached with three small screws that thread into sheet metal above the headliner. The visor flap is usually a piece of pressed board with an attached piece of metal that slides over the mounting bracket. The bend in the mounting bracket allows the visor flap to stay in the desired position. An un-upholstered visor flap serves its intended function just fine, but it looks unfinished.

Sun visor mounting brackets are not universal in fit, but you can find suitable replacements for similar vehicles of different makes from the same manufacturer. So if your sun visors are missing or damaged beyond repair, you can probably find the essentials in a salvage yard. As long as you have the mounting bracket and the portion of the flap that slides over the mounting bracket, you can make your own visor flap out of particle board, Masonite, plywood, or even aluminum, as long as the material is about 3/16-inch thick.

Once you have a visor flap, wrap it with the material of your choice and simply sew the raw edges together. You can even attach some padding to the flap prior to wrapping it.

A withered sunvisor can easily ruin an otherwise beautifully upholstered vehicle—don't overlook an eyesore like this.

Glove Box

What can you do to the glove box to make it look better? For one, take everything but gloves out of it. This includes any ketchup and salt packets from the fast-food restaurant, unpaid parking tickets, and the directions to last week's party. After you have everything out of the glove box, clean it out with a vacuum or a whisk broom.

The actual box portion of most glove boxes is made of cardboard that is folded and stapled into the proper shape. You may find the box to be stretched, torn, or damaged from long-term use. Though not crucial, replacing the glove box incurs minimum cost when compared to other custom interior work, and you'll have one more finished detail that contributes to the whole package.

Kick Panels

In the world of auto upholstery customization, kick panels are often forgotten and get the dirty end of the deal. Since they are located under the dash and in front of the door panels, they fall into the "out of sight, out of mind" category. If you happen to have mud, dirt, or grease on your shoes or pants leg, it ends up on the kick panels in addition to the carpeting or floor mats. Hard plastic or vinyl kick panels are also susceptible to being scratched, gouged, or marred by shoes or anything else hauled in from the passenger seat. Older vehicles often have kick panels made from cardboard. These panels are easily damaged by moisture soaked up from the carpeting or leaked through the window.

To thoroughly inspect your kick panels, remove them from the vehicle. They are usually held in place by two or three small screws, making their removal easy. If they are cardboard-based and damaged by moisture, they need to be replaced. Replacement kick panels are available for many vehicles and are easy to make if replacements for your vehicle are not available. Begin by making a pattern of the area you wish to cover. Be sure to include the locations for mounting holes, stereo speakers, or vents. When you have the pattern cut to the correct size and shape, transfer it to a piece of panel board or Masonite.

Test fit the kick panel to the door, making sure the holes for mounting screws are properly aligned. If your kick panel has a three-dimensional pattern, use reference marks to ensure proper alignment of each layer of foam padding material.

When the kick panel is cut to the appropriate size and shaped as desired, it needs to be covered with foam padding. Cut a piece of 1/4- or 3/8-inch-thick foam padding large enough to cover the entire kick panel. Spray the back of the foam padding and the front of the kick panel with spray adhesive. Position the foam padding on the kick panel and press it into place. Start in the middle and work toward the edges, making sure that all wrinkles are pressed out of the foam. Cut off any excess foam padding at the edge of the kick panel.

Cut a piece of fabric (tweed, vinyl, and leather work best) large enough to cover the kick panel, plus an inch or two around all edges. Fold the fabric over on itself and spray the back of one half with spray adhesive. Spray the appropriate portion of the kick panel with spray adhesive and allow it to become tacky. Making sure the fabric extends past the edges of the panel, press the fabric into place. Working outward from the middle, press out any wrinkles in the fabric. Make sure the fabric makes good contact with the foam padding over the entire surface area. Apply spray adhesive to the back of the remaining half of the fabric and to the front of the remainder of the kick panel, then press the fabric into place. When you are finished with the front side of the kick panel, apply spray adhesive to the back of the kick panel and to the back of the remaining material. Wrap the material over the edge of the kick panel and press it into place on the back.

If your kick panels are made of plastic and are in decent condition other than being faded, repaint them to bring them up to the standards of your new interior. First wash the parts to be painted with warm soapy water and a small scrub brush. Kick panels are often the filthiest pieces in the interior of a vehicle, so they might require some good scrubbing. Rinse the pieces thoroughly with clean water. If they still look dirty, scrub them again with a new batch of soapy water. Wipe the parts with wax and grease remover and wipe them dry with a clean cloth. Apply primer according to the manufacturer's instructions. After the appropriate drying time, apply a complementary coat of paint, also following the manufacturer's instructions.

Window Run Channels

Window run channels are felt-lined grooves that keep the top and edges of window glass from moving and rattling around while the vehicle is moving. If you are simply performing upholstery work on the vehicle and the existing window run channels are in good shape, replacing them is up to you. However, if the vehicle is going through a complete makeover and the doors are going to be repainted, the window run channels should be replaced. The decision to do this should be made prior to painting the doors, so you can paint any area that will not be covered by new window run channels.

A window run channel is installed by sliding one end down into the back of the door and then pressing the channel into place up, around the top of the door, and down again to the front of the door. Each end of the channel is held in place by a clip built into the inside of the door. In some vehicles, window run channels are secured with additional small flathead screws.

Without a run channel, the window is easily scratched and your car cheapened. Replacing them is one of the easiest accessory repairs.

Garnish Moldings

Most vehicles manufactured before the 1960s used garnish moldings around the inside of the windshield, rear glass, and door windows. In addition to covering the molding or sealer securing the glass, garnish moldings cover the edges of door panels and headliners. They are usually held in place with screws, so their removal and installation is straightforward.

At the factory, most garnish moldings are painted if they are metal or, on newer vehicles, molded in the same color as the rest of the vinyl interior panels. Vinyl garnish moldings can be repainted in the color of your choice using paint designed especially for vinyl products.

If the garnish moldings are made of metal (sheet metal, aluminum, or stainless steel are common), your choice of finishes is somewhat larger. To match the rest of the new interior, upholster the garnish molding with similar material. Cut a strip of material slightly longer than the entire perimeter of the garnish molding and about 1 inch wider. Apply spray adhesive to the back of the material and to the face of the garnish molding. Press the material into place on the face of the molding, beginning with one end of the material at the center of the top portion of the garnish molding. Smooth out wrinkles as you work your way around the molding and make sure the material extends past both edges. When you get back to where you started, you have two choices of how to finish. You can cut the material so that both ends are flush, but if the material shrinks, there will be a gap. A better way to terminate the covering is to allow the end to overlap the beginning by 1/2 inch. This measurement isn't a magical number; it can be whatever you want it to be, but it should be consistent on all garnish moldings. After the face of the molding is covered, apply a bit more spray adhesive to the back of the material and the garnish molding. Press the edges of material firmly into place on the back of the molding. Trim off all but about 1/4 inch of material from the back to allow the garnish molding to fit properly. Metal garnish moldings can be painted to match or complement other painted sections of the interior. Prior to painting any surface of an automobile, clean it with wax and grease remover. Sand away any scratches or imperfections with a Scotch-Brite pad. Clean the garnish moldings again with wax and grease remover (wiped on with one cloth and dried with a clean cloth). Apply the appropriate primer and paint following the manufacturer's directions for application, drying time, and safety.

Aluminum or stainless-steel garnish moldings (or any other interior trim) can be painted, but you can add some sparkle by polishing it. Use a Dremel tool or a similar rotary tool with various polishing compounds to make the surfaces look like chrome. Of course, a chrome-plated metal garnish molding is an option too. To obtain the look of billet aluminum, scuff aluminum trim with a Scotch-Brite pad and protect it with a coat or two of clear paint. Another option for aluminum trim is to have it anodized any of a variety of colors. This is less common on garnish moldings.

Rubber Weather Stripping

Any insulation in a vehicle will be ineffective if the rubber weather stripping is missing or damaged. For all intents and purposes, it is impossible to make a functional automobile door that also seals completely. This makes weather stripping a necessity if you want to keep weather and noise out. Weather stripping comes in a multitude of types for a variety of applications. Most suppliers can provide samples or drawings to give you an idea what to purchase.

Determine first if the weather stripping should be located on the door or in the doorjamb. Measure around the perimeter where the weather stripping will be applied and order an extra foot for each piece you need. Clean the surface where the weather stripping will be applied with wax and grease remover. Apply a bead of 3M Weatherstrip Adhesive to the back of the weather stripping and press it into place. Use strips of masking tape approximately 1 foot apart all the way around the length of the weather stripping to hold it in place until the adhesive sets.

Package Trays

The package tray, the large area behind the rear seat, can be damaged by heat from the sun being magnified through the rear window. Some package trays are made of an un-upholstered textured composite material. Some are made of sheet metal that has been painted or covered with vinyl. Damaged trays need to be replaced. Mounting methods vary for each vehicle, so consult a repair manual for your specific vehicle for removal and replacement instructions.

With the old tray out of the car or before you install a replacement, you might want to cover the tray with material to match the rest of your newly upholstered vehicle. Pull the tray out of the vehicle, so it's easier to make a pattern. Make a pattern from Kraft paper or simply lay the package tray onto a piece of 1/4-inch or 3/16-inch foam and cut around it with a razor knife. Lay the package tray onto the material you plan to cover it with and draw a line around the tray about 1 inch away from the edges. Spray the back of the upholstery material and the top of the foam with spray adhesive. Position the upholstery material on the package tray so that there is overlap on all sides. Smooth out the material with your hands. Wrap the edges of the package tray with the excess material, securing it to the back with more spray adhesive as necessary. You can now reinstall the package tray.

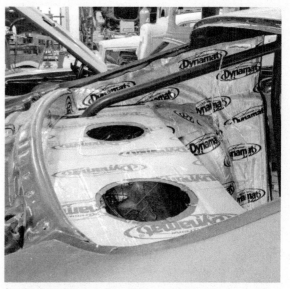

Covering the package tray with matching material as the rest of your vehicle helps complete the picture of a fully-upholstered and custom vehicle.

PROJECT 12
Covering a Trunk Speaker Box

Time: 1–2 hours

Skill Level: Easy

Cost: Low

Tools & Materials: MDF (medium-density fiberboard) or preferred material for speakerbox, glue, pneumatic stapler, utility knife, shears, electric drill, screws, polyester fiber filler (optional), preferred carpet material

Speaker enclosures can be extensive or simple. This one is relatively simple, which makes good sense since it is going in an early 1990s Ford Mustang, a vehicle driven daily.

A one-off hot rod, custom car, or show car might call for something more elaborate, but for this vehicle, a simple box serves quite well.

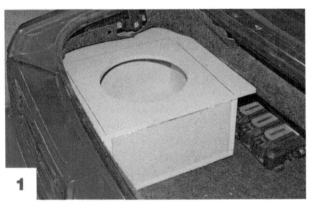

1

Perhaps the most difficult task is designing the component housing. Here, a square box has been fashioned from MDF. The top is slightly larger on the sides adjacent to the rear quarter panel and the front of the trunk. The cantilevered top closes off the trunk to the side and still allows for some storage room in the front.

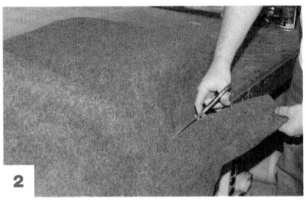

2

With the box constructed (glued and stapled together), cut a piece of carpet that matches the rest of the trunk carpeting.

3

A square edge on the MDF would quickly wear through the carpeting, so use a router to form a smooth round edge.

4

This is how the speaker enclosure will be oriented in the driver side of the trunk when viewed from the outside. The speaker will be mounted in the hole in the top of the enclosure. In this photo, it is difficult to see the angled piece of MDF that fills the gap between the top overhang and the front of the box.

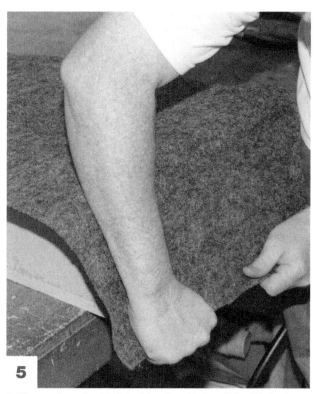

5

Pull the carpet over the side that will be adjacent to the middle of the trunk space. Use a pneumatic stapler to secure the carpet to the bottom of the speaker enclosure.

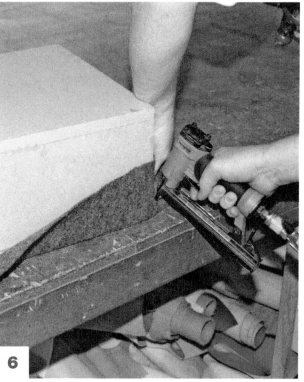

6

Pull the carpet across the top and staple it to the bottom of the cantilevered top that will be located near the quarter panel of the vehicle. Cover the top edge with carpet and staple it in place.

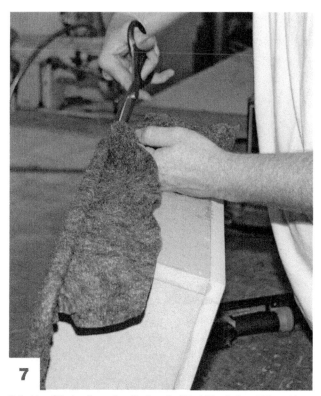

7

Both sides of the box (forward and backward) will be hidden in the vehicle, so trim away any excess carpeting below the bottom edge of the top.

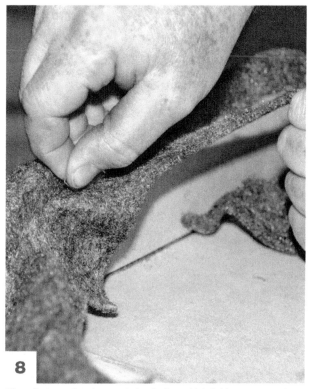

8

Where shears won't work, use a single-edged razor blade to trim excess carpet from the cantilevered top.

9

Use a single-edged razor blade to trim away carpet at the opening for the speaker.

10

Drill a hole for the speaker wires to pass through in an inconspicuous location on the side of the box. To improve sound from the speaker, fill the speaker enclosure with polyester fiber filler.

11

Position the speaker so its flange rests on the top face of the enclosure. Put screws through the flange into the top panel to secure the speaker in place.

12

Easily covered, the speaker enclosure looks great. All that is left is to run the wires to the stereo or amplifier and then crank it up.

PROJECT 13
Covering the Inside of a Deck Lid

 Time: 2–4 hours

 Skill Level: Medium

 Cost: Low–Medium

 Tools & Materials: Panel board, electric drill, screws, compass, sandpaper, leather punch, closed-cell foam, utility knife, razor blade, shears, plastic fasteners, spray adhesive, pneumatic stapler, dowel, preferred cover material

The interior panels for a trunk are made in much the same fashion as door panels. A slightly different process is followed for covering the inside of a deck lid. It is a fairly simple process, and the photos make it even easier to understand. While this upholstered panel is not extravagant, it does help finish the trunk space, making it a worthy endeavor.

Instead of just throwing the spare tire and jack in the trunk, stow them in their designated locations and secure them as designed. This eliminates annoying rattles and puts emergency tools where you can find them. An emergency toolkit, a first-aid kit, and safety items are acceptable in the trunk, but eliminate empty beverage cans, chip bags, and any other trash. Use a heavy-duty vacuum cleaner or shop vacuum to remove all the dust, dirt, and debris from the trunk. Depending on the size of the trunk, you can fabricate and cover some vertical panels to conceal storage space and give the trunk a finished look.

Unless you are going to use the trunk as intended (to carry a spare tire, groceries, and luggage), it might as well be finished as nicely as the rest of the vehicle.

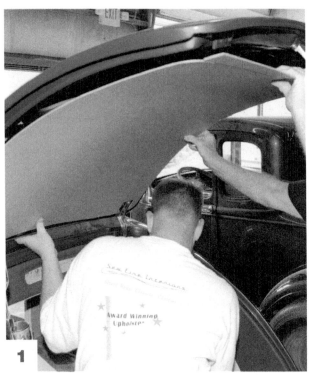

1 With the panel board mostly roughed out, the template still requires a few simple tweaks. Most deck lid inner skins have both raised and recessed areas. For the most part, the panel will cover the outermost raised area, with notches cut for the hinges, the latch, and the prop rod.

2 With the panel board held in place by an assistant, use a hand drill and short screws to secure the panel board to the inside of the deck lid. These screws will be replaced later. Use screws that are not too long, so they don't go through the outside of the deck lid. Otherwise, you'll be paying a body and paint guy to fix your mistake.

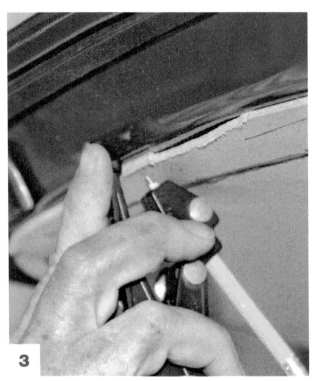

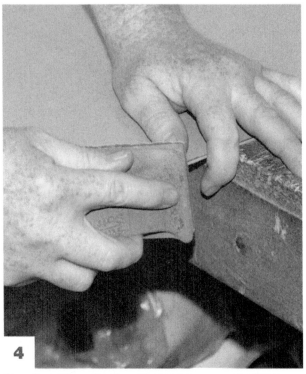

3 A compass attachment allows you to draw lines offset from a body line or whatever you slide the compass along, allowing you to copy the shape of the outer rim of the deck lid's raised panel onto the panel board.

4 After cutting out the panel board, use 80-grit sandpaper on a sanding block to smooth the edges. Rough edges tend to wear through the upholstery. A smooth edge is infinitely superior.

5

At each mounting hole, use a leather punch to make a larger hole in the pattern board. Plastic fasteners will eventually be inserted into these holes. It is important that the holes and fasteners are compatible sizes.

6

Lay the panel board atop a piece of 1/2-inch-thick closed-cell foam. Next, cut a piece of foam large enough to cover the panel board.

7

Using a spray gun, apply spray adhesive to the front of the panel board.

8

Apply spray adhesive to the back of the closed-cell foam.

9

Place the panel board face-down on the glued face of the closed-cell foam. It is not necessary to use a roller, but at least use your hands to firmly press the panel board onto the foam. Verify that good contact is made over the entire panel.

10

Use a single-edged razor blade from the underside to trim the foam to the correct size and shape. Recesses for the hinges, latch, and prop rod need to be cut, but nothing is required at the mounting-hole locations.

11

Use a pair of shears to cut a piece of upholstery large enough to cover the inside of the deck lid.

12

Closed-cell foam has a slightly slick surface, so prior to applying spray adhesive, use 80-grit sandpaper on a sanding block to rough up the surface slightly.

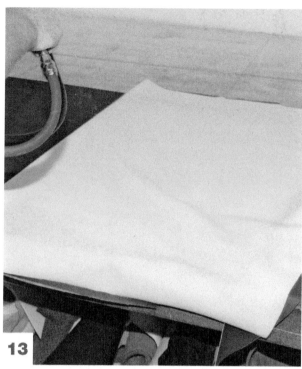

13 Lay the upholstery material (vinyl in this case) over the foam-covered panel board, verifying that the vinyl covers the entire board. Fold over approximately half the vinyl and apply spray adhesive to the front and back of the foam.

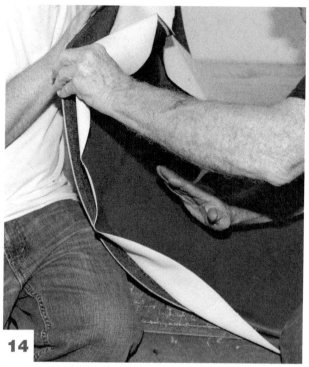

14 Press the vinyl onto the closed-cell foam. Fold the remaining vinyl back and apply spray adhesive to the back of the vinyl and the front of the remaining foam. Press the vinyl into place. Since the lower portion of the deck lid is curved, hold the panel in approximately the same way direction as a helper presses the vinyl into place. This ensures that the vinyl and foam make good contact, minimizing the chance of sagging material long after the work is done.

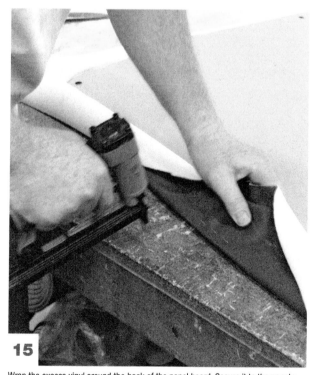

15 Wrap the excess vinyl around the back of the panel board. Secure it to the panel board with staples spaced about 1/4 inch apart.

16 Using a single-edged razor blade, cut off any excess material just past the row of staples. The bow in the line of staples is to allow for insertion of a plastic fastener.

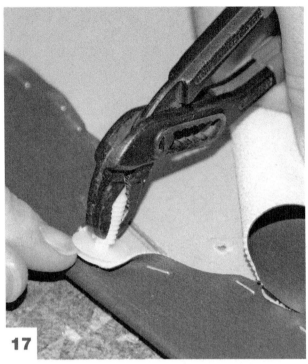

17

These plastic fasteners (aka Christmas trees) have a pair of round, flat surfaces approximately 1/8 inch apart along the shaft, with multiple rings of decreasing size serving as branches. On the outermost round surface, approximately a quarter of the round is left off, allowing the user to thread the fastener onto the panel board. The branches of the tree fit into the mounting holes in the deck lid.

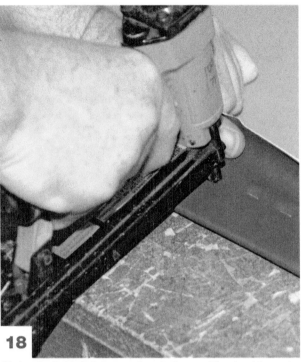

18

After inserting the plastic fastener, continue stapling around the edge of the panel board, inserting staples approximately 1/4 inch apart, with another plastic fastener at each mounting point.

19

Glue the vinyl to the front of the foam-covered panel board, wrapping the edges around to the back, stapled and trimmed, with plastic fasteners installed.

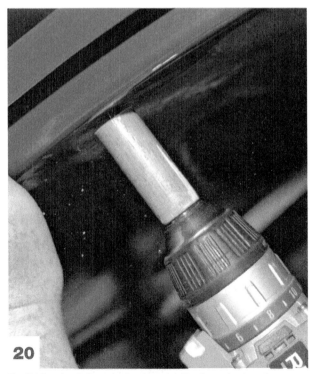

20

The Christmas tree fasteners require a larger hole than the previously used screws. Use a drill bit of the appropriate size to enlarge the holes. Use a solid dowel with a hole in it as a depth guard to prevent the drill from slipping and going through the deck lid.

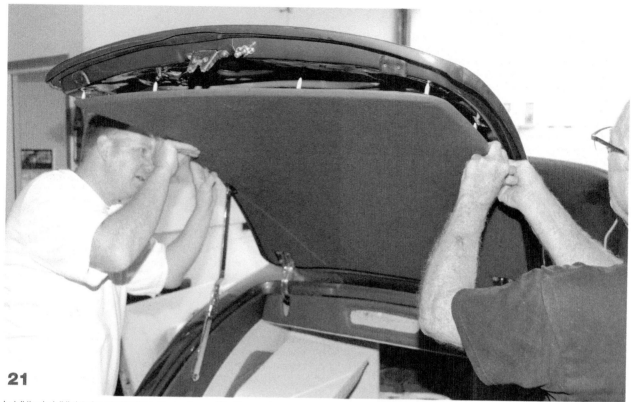

21

Install the deck lid's interior panel by fitting the panel around the hinges and pressing the plastic fasteners into their respective holes.

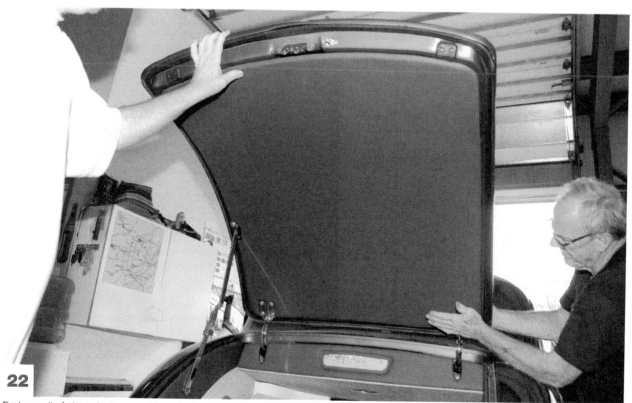

22

Firmly press the fasteners in place around the perimeter of the deck lid, verifying that they are properly seated. This particular panel is nothing fancy, but it goes a long way toward finishing the trunk area.

APPENDIX

Upholstery Maintenance

When people pick up a vehicle with a freshly upholstered interior, they often ask how to maintain its new appearance. Many upholsterers give customers a list of recommended products and any other cleaning/maintenance information.

The following recommendations are strictly that—recommendations. You may find other products that work equally as well or even better. Whatever works best for you is what I recommend you use. Remember that regular cleaning, regardless of what you use, will keep your upholstery looking fresher and lasting longer.

CLEANING

Since the interiors of vehicles are usually covered with a variety of materials, no one product is going to be best for cleaning and protecting all freshly upholstered surfaces. You will need to determine what kind of material needs to be cleaned and then use the best product for that material.

Fabric Surfaces: Fabric surfaces include tweed, mohair, cloth, velvet, and burlap. Due to the relatively coarse nature of these fabrics, they are the most difficult to clean and keep clean. Use a vacuum cleaner to pull dust, dirt, and grit out of these materials. Avoid aggressively wiping dust, dirt, or spilled items off fabric, as this will actually just grind the substance into the fabric. Liquids such as soda can be soaked up with a dry towel. Clean the surface with a damp towel.

Leather and Vinyl Surfaces: Leather and vinyl are much easier to keep clean, making them popular materials for automotive upholstery. Accumulations of dry substances (dirt, sand, ashes) can be vacuumed from these surfaces, while small amounts can be wiped away with a dry cloth. If small particles remain after wiping, use a damp cloth to clean up any residue. Avoid using a soaking-wet cloth. Lint-free Armor All Cleaning Wipes work well for cleaning vinyl surfaces, while Armor-All Leather Wipes are more suitable for leather surfaces. Do not use these products on painted or glass surfaces. The silicone in Armor All products will make it difficult for paint to stick if the surface ever needs to be painted, and it causes clouding on glass surfaces.

Plastic Surfaces: For cleaning most plastic surfaces, plain soap and water, and a sponge or soft cloth, work well. Add a few squirts of liquid dishwashing detergent to 1 gallon of warm water. For stubborn stains, Simple Green or Fast Orange (or comparable cleaners) squirted onto a soft cloth might be necessary. It may take a while (and your elbow and shoulder might get sore before you are done), but these products will usually work. If they don't, consider repainting the plastic.

Chrome and Stainless-Steel Surfaces: Chrome and stainless-steel trim are usually cleaned with a damp cloth, provided their surfaces are smooth. Textured surfaces may require a soft brush to get dirt out of crevices. Substances that cannot be removed by these procedures can be removed from stainless steel with a piece of very fine steel wool. Chrome polish usually removes the most stubborn stains from chrome.

Do not mistake chromed plastic for stainless steel. If you use an abrasive on chromed plastic, you'll remove the finish.

Painted Surfaces: Painted surfaces are cleaned with soap and water or with Simple Green or Fast Orange, just like plastic surfaces. Avoid using any sort of abrasive, as it will scratch the paint and could eventually lead to the formation of rust.

Carpet Surfaces: Frequent vacuuming is the best way to keep carpeted areas clean. A shop vacuum is a handy accessory to have in your garage. If you don't have one, most car washes have vacuums that cost less than a dollar or two per use. If you do have a shop vac, spend a few extra bucks to get an attachment for cleaning crevices. This will make it easier to clean between the seat cushion and seat back, as well as between all the nooks and crannies between seats and cushions.

Glass Surfaces: Fresh newspaper and a liquid glass cleaner are best for keeping the glass in your vehicle clean. Wipe in a horizontal direction on one side of the glass and in a vertical direction on the opposite side to determine where the streaks are located.

PROTECTING

Like a good coat of wax on a vehicle's exterior, using the appropriate products on the interior will help keep it clean. When the inevitable spill occurs, damage to the interior will be minimized.

Fabric Surfaces: Scotchgard is a spray-on treatment that helps keep liquids and dirt from penetrating into fabric surfaces. This treatment is available from some auto dealers and aftermarket dealers but can also be purchased in aerosol cans for the do-it-yourselfer.

Leather and Vinyl Surfaces: Leather care products are available at most leading auto parts stores. Although similar products have come along, I use Armor All wipes or spray to keep vinyl surfaces clean. Avoid using this product on painted surfaces or glass.

Chrome and Stainless-Steel Surfaces: Most major auto parts stores and discount stores with an auto accessories department have a multitude of chrome and stainless-steel polishes and rubbing compounds. Pick one that suits your needs and apply it according to the directions. Note that rubbing compounds are abrasive, so be sure to read the fine print on the label to make sure the product is right for you.

Painted Surfaces: As with the exterior of your vehicle, it's good to apply paste wax to all painted surfaces on the interior. Exceptions are any antiglare surfaces and the steering wheel.

Carpet Surfaces: Carpeted floors are subjected to most everything imaginable, including our feet. For this reason, a set of floor mats is essential for keeping the carpet in your vehicle looking decent. Vinyl floor mats that can be removed and sprayed with a hose or scrubbed with a brush are the easiest to keep clean. Carpeted floor mats look nicer but are not much easier to keep clean than the rest of the carpeting on the floor. Their saving grace is that for the most part, they will protect the carpet beneath them and can be replaced when they look too bad.

Resources

Appleman Interiors
4620 Lancaster-Kirkersville Road
Lancaster, OH 43130
740-756-4295
Custom automotive upholstery

Auto Custom Carpets, Inc.
P.O. Box 1350
Anniston, AL 36202
www.accmats.com
800-352-8216
OEM and custom carpeting

C.A.R.S. Inc.
2600 Bond Street
Rochester Hills, MI 48309
www.carsinc.com
800-CARS INC
Chevrolet restoration products

Cerullo
2881 Metropolitan Place
Pomona, CA 91767
www.cerullo.com
909-392-5561
Ready-to-install custom seats

Chevs of the 40s
1605 NE 112th Street
Vancouver, WA 98686
www.chevsofthe40s.com
877-735-0587
Chevrolet restoration products

Classic Industries, Inc.
18460 Gothard Street
Huntington Beach, CA 92648
www.classicindustries.com
800-854-1280
Distributor of reproduction and
original GM parts and accessories

Convertible Service
5126 R. Walnut Grove Avenue
San Gabriel, CA 91776
www.convertibleparts.com
800-333-1140
Full line of convertible parts for vehicles
from 1946 to the present

Danchuk Manufacturing
3201 S. Standard Avenue
Santa Ana, CA 92705
and
8599 Motorsports Way
Brownsburg, IN 46112
www.danchuk.com
800-648-9554
Chevrolet restoration products

Don Albers Upholstery
5 Lone Eagle Trail
St. Charles, MO 63303
636-441-2007
Custom automotive upholstery

Dynamic Control of North America, Inc.
3042 Symmes Road
Hamilton, OH 45015
www.dynamat.com
513-860-5094
Dynamat sound-deadening and
insulation products

EZ Boy Interiors
6 Chestnut Street
Amesbury, MA 01913
www.ezboyinteriors.com
800-423-6053
Seat frames, seat covers, carpeting,
headliners

Fryer's Auto Upholstery Kits
15025 Twenty-second Avenue NW
Marysville, WA 98271
www.autoupholsterykits.com
888-205-4659
Automotive upholstery kits

The Glass House
446 W. Arrow Highway, no. 4
San Dimas, CA 91773
www.theglasshouse1.com
866-415-5982
Windshield glass, weather stripping,
and other glass-related items

Glide Engineering
10662 Pullman Court
Rancho Cucamonga, CA 91730
www.glideengineering.com
800-301-3334
Seat frames and covers

Goodmark Industries, Inc.
305 Shawnee North Drive, Suite 450
Suwanee, GA 30024
www.goodmarkindustries.com
770-339-8557
Restoration body panels and trim

Haartz Corporation
87 Haywood Road
Action, MA 01720
www.haartz.com
978-264-2600
Convertible top and tonneau cover
material

HushMat
15032 W. 117th Street
Olathe, KS 66062
www.hushmat.com
913-599-2600
HushMat sound-deadening and
insulation products

KS Reproduction Corporation
100A Wade Avenue
South Plainfield, NJ 07080
www.ksreproduction.com
800-445-4540
Manufacturer of restoration and
reproduction parts

LeBaron Bonney
6 Chestnut Street
Amesbury, MA 01913
www.lebaronbonney.com
800-221-5408
Ford interior upholstery, tops, and
accessories

Meissner Sewing Machine Company
2417 Cormorant Way
Sacramento, CA 95815
www.meissnersewing.com
916-920-2121
Industrial-quality sewing machines and supplies

National Fabric Company, Inc.
901 South Seventh Street
Kansas City, KS 66105
913-281-1833
Upholstery fabric and supplies

National Parts Depot
900 SW Thirty-eighth Avenue
Ocala, FL 34474
www.npdlink.com
352-861-8700
Restoration and reproduction parts

Original Parts Group
1770 Saturn Way
Seal Beach, CA 90740
www.opgi.com
800-243-8355
GM restoration parts

Phipps Rod & Custom Accessories, Inc.
9961 Apache Boulevard
West Palm Beach, FL 33412
www.phippsproducts.com
866-744-7771
Custom interior products and custom upholstery

Quality Industrial Sewing Machines
2921 West Stolley Park Road
Grand Island, NE 68801
www.qualitysew.com
800-431-0032
Sewing machines and upholstery supplies

Restoration Specialties & Supply
P.O. Box 328
Windber, PA 15963
www.restorationspecialties.com
814-467-9842
Upholstery supplies

Sam Wright Hot Rod Interiors
304 East 1400 Road
Baldwin City, KS 66006
785-594-7430
Custom automotive upholstery

Sew Fine Interiors
4178 Shady Springs Lane
St. Peters, MO 63376
www.sewfineinteriors.com
636-922-1222
Custom automotive upholstery

Sid Chavers Company
880 Aldo Avenue
Santa Clara, CA 95054
www.sidchaverscompany.com
408-980-9081
Custom automotive upholstery

Street Rod Interiors
6121 Midway Road
Fort Worth, TX 76117
www.larrydennis.com
800-772-7542
Upholstery tools and supplies

Tea's Design, Inc.
1177 Chester Avenue SE
Rochester, MN 55904
www.teasdesign.com
800-791-7328
Ready-to-install bench, bucket, or split bench seats

Trim Parts
2175 Deerfield Road
Lebanon, OH 45036
www.trimparts.com
513-934-0815
Custom-molded carpets and interior trim

Wholesale USA, Inc.
10729 Trenton Avenue
St. Louis, MO 63132
www.wholesaleusastl.com
314-427-2400
Upholstery fabric and supplies

Wise Guys
P.O. Box 211
Elkhart, IN 46515
www.wiseguys-seats.com
866-494-7348
Seat frames and accessories

Summary

Upholstery is probably the last item that do-it-yourselfer car guys would consider attempting. Many do not hesitate to grab a welding torch and create a vehicle chassis with nothing but some steel tubing and welding rod. Others don't bat an eye at the challenge of painting a vehicle or wiring one from scratch. But when it comes to upholstery, many a hot rodder is stopped dead in his tracks at the mere thought. While upholstery isn't for everyone, you won't know until you try.

It is highly unlikely that I will purchase an industrial-quality sewing machine, so I won't be doing any sewing anytime soon. However, in my upcoming 1955 Chevrolet pickup project, I plan to do a fair amount of upholstery-related work myself. I have chosen to install a set of aftermarket bucket seats in the truck. From the knowledge I have gained writing this book, I think I can fabricate and cover a center console and door panels. I'll also most likely install the insulation and sound-deadening material, along with carpet padding and the carpet itself. Doing these tasks myself will undoubtedly save me a little money, but the personal rewards from a job well done are much more valuable than a few extra nickels.

Whether you perform any or all these tasks yourself is up to you. However, I hope I have provided you with enough insight to make informed decisions as to whether or not you can do it yourself. If you are up to the challenge and are willing to make an attempt, this book will not only tell you but also show you how upholstery tasks are performed. If you save some money on your next project by doing it yourself, that is great. If you become the go-to guy for upholstery among your friends, that is even better. If you begin making a living by practicing what you have learned in this book, please let me know, and I wish you well in your future upholstery projects.

About the Author

How to Restore and Customize Auto Interiors is the eleventh book from author Dennis W. Parks. Parks has been a freelance automotive photojournalist since 1985. His other books include How to Paint Your Car, How to Build a Hot Rod with Boyd Coddington, How to Restore and Customize Auto Upholstery and Interiors, How to Plate, Polish and Chrome, How to Build a Cheap Hot Rod, The Complete Guide to Auto Body Repair, Hot Rod Body and Chassis Builder's Guide, and Automotive Wiring. Parks' writing and photography have appeared in Street Rodder, Hot Rod, Midwest Rod & Machine, Truckin', Rodder's Digest, Street Rod Action, Custom Rodder, Rod & Custom, Super Chevy, Custom Classic Trucks, American Rodder, and High Performance Pontiac magazines.

Parks is the cofounder and editor in chief of Hot Rod Garage, LLC, an authoritative hot rod website (www.hot-rod-garage.com). He lives outside St. Louis, Missouri. He is currently rebuilding a 1955 Chevy pickup.

The author alongside his 1927 Ford Track T roadster. Construction of the Track T was documented in *How to Build a Cheap Hot Rod* and *Hot Rod Body and Chassis Builder's Guide*.

Index

CPSIA information can be obtained
at www.ICGtesting.com
Printed in the USA
LVOW05s1553100216

474388LV00006B/7/P